Matthew Eckert

LETTERS TO GARRET

Practical Lessons
for Life-on-Life Christian Discipleship

Copyright © 2014 by Matthew Eckert
First Edition – July 2014

ISBN
978-1-4602-4368-8 (Hardcover)
978-1-4602-4369-5 (Paperback)
978-1-4602-4370-1 (eBook)

All rights reserved.

No part of this publication may be reproduced in any form, or by any means, electronic or mechanical, including photocopying, recording, or any information browsing, storage, or retrieval system, without permission in writing from the publisher.

Produced by:

FriesenPress

Suite 300 – 852 Fort Street
Victoria, BC, Canada V8W 1H8

www.friesenpress.com

Distributed to the trade by The Ingram Book Company

TABLE OF CONTENTS

Foreword	v
Preface	ix
Introduction	xiii
Acknowledgements	xxi
Letter of Introduction	1
Fear	5
It's all about time	9
Conversations	13
Lead, don't facilitate	15
Scripture Memory	17
Stay focused	21
Obedience to the process	23
Curriculum	27
It's all about love	31
Questions	33
Prayer	35
Rhythms	37
Keep learning	39
Reflection	41
Time for Transformation	43
Scripture	47
Complexity	51
Theological thinking	53
Uniqueness of each person	55
Messy journey	57
Personal confession	61
Learning process	63
Be a Luch to someone	65

The hermeneutical spiral	67
Funerals	71
Minimum requirements	73
Diversity	75
Don't facilitate	77
Defining success	79
Summer vacation	83
Who to invest in	87
The fear of change	89
It's all about the core	93
More thoughts on reflecting	95
Don't lead like Jesus	99
Discipleship is not simple	101
Do what you already know is right	105
Fragile	109
Dear Reader of "Letters to Garret",	113
About the Author	117

FOREWORD

In the fall of 1986, I was immersed in campus ministry at the University of Guelph. I was equipped, trained, and on fire to fulfill the Great Commission. I was eager to make a permanent difference in the lives of young adults. I had a burning passion to not just be busy doing church work, but to heed the call to do the work of the Church, which really is the work of expressing and extending the Kingdom of God in the lives of people.

Armed with a simple conviction that only two things last forever—the Word of God and the souls of people—I was praying day and night that God would use me to raise up a new generation of disciples and labourers, who would go far beyond my limited reach. I had a desire to see people populate the planet who would express the life of Jesus in every dimension and sphere of their lives—their studies, their home life, their personal life, and eventually their own families and careers.

During that era of my life, I had a profile of the kind of person I wanted to invest my life in. It consisted of the acronym F.A.I.T.H. I was looking for men and women who were:

> Faithful—those who would keep their word

> Available—they were there to play not just spectate

Initiators—they didn't have to be coaxed to grow; they were eager to do so

Teachable—they were hungry to learn, grow, and yearned for feedback

Heart for God—most importantly, they had a growing appetite for God's presence

Enter Matthew Eckert.

I was invited to speak to a youth leaders' conference. I believe I was speaking on having a heart for people, for individuals, to invest our lives in them in obedience to the Great Commission. During one of the breaks, a good-looking young man, tall, with blond hair and striking blue eyes, presented himself to me and said, "Hi, my name is Matthew Eckert. I am a second year student at the University of Guelph and you are going to be my mentor." I thought, 'who is this guy?' I didn't actually say it to him, but I thought, 'Man this guy has the nerve, but he sure is bold, and I like that."

We decided to meet up the following week on campus and that began a three year journey together of me as 'the older guy' walking alongside this young man who was clearly eager to grow in the things of God.

One of the first things I noticed about Matthew was that he wasn't big on groups, especially if he thought the groups weren't doing anything big or going anywhere special. At that time, I wanted to build a community of growing disciples, and Matthew was not one to fit into someone else's program of discipleship. It became apparent to me really fast that if I wanted to impact this young man's life, it would require a healthy dose of creativity and availability on my part.

And that's what I did. Although Matthew is now big on having a structured approach with sound curriculum, back then he balked at anything that made him feel like he was being cloned or herded. Knowing what I wanted to pass on to him, I kept that in the back of my mind. As we began to meet, I would WOLEP Matthew—share the Word appropriately, Observe him, Listen deeply, Encourage him and Pray for and with him. Not in any particular order, but just as the need presented itself.

I began to intentionally disciple Matthew based on his needs, not mine.

After Matthew graduated from university and from the custom designed approach to discipling him that I had created, he went on to work out the principles of his own. This began in his work as a banker, then later in his present work as a pastor with an exceptional commitment to people development.

You will have to dive into this manual to uncover some of the intentional lessons that we worked through. What you will find, I hope, as Matthew has, that there is no set formula for making disciples. The most important things, as Matthew so adeptly lays out, are passing on to a disciple a working knowledge of the Scriptures, modeling the disciplines and habits of a disciple's life, and often doing life together in the context of a mutual friendship, but understanding that one is the mentor and the other is in the place of being mentored.

As you will see throughout this excellent book, Matthew mastered those early lessons and in this creative framework of letters to a disciple he calls Garret, Matthew has laid out a blueprint in the spirit and wisdom of the apostle Paul in 1 Corinthians 3:10-15

[10] According to the grace of God given to me, like a skilled master builder I laid a foundation, and someone else is building upon it. Let each one take care how he builds upon it. [11] For no one can lay a foundation other than that which is laid, which is Jesus Christ. [12] Now if anyone builds on the foundation with gold, silver, precious stones, wood, hay, straw— [13] each one's work will become manifest, for the Day will disclose it, because it will be revealed by fire, and the fire will test what sort of work each one has done. [14] If the work that anyone has built on the foundation

survives, he will receive a reward. [15] If anyone's work is burned up, he will suffer loss, though he himself will be saved, but only as through fire.

Throughout this good work, Matthew has been careful to lay out some fundamentals that anyone aspiring to build into the lives of people can use. You can be a veteran disciple-maker, a people builder like me, or you can be just starting out. Matthew has done a great job of laying out the basics in the spirit of the skilled master builder Paul speaks of.

One thing that will be evident throughout this book is that Matthew, although having been a business man and now a pastor and academic, has never lost his zeal and passion and clarity about investing in the lives of a few men and women. What is exciting for me is to see him passing on this same vision to his adult children and seeing them carry the baton forward.

As I have watched Matthew mature in his theological precision around this theme of the Great Commission and his absolute focus on discipling a few, I am encouraged that you are holding in your hands a tool that you will find yourself coming back to over and over again as you pick up the baton and run with it.

Matthew honours me in one chapter in which he speaks of being a Luch to someone, meaning do for someone else what Luch did for him.

Well, it is my privilege to be able to bless you, the reader, and encourage you to be a Matthew to someone as you join the adventure of a lifetime of disciple-making.

Luciano Del Monte
Guelph, Ontario, Canada

PREFACE

I WAS TWENTY YEARS OLD, IN MY SECOND YEAR AT the University of Guelph, in Ontario, Canada. Living away from home and the church context I was familiar with, I was looking to solidify my faith. But how do you do this? Post high school years are a time when many leave the faith of their youth – it is that way today and it was that way when I was in university in the mid-1980s.

I was part of a Christian campus group during my first year, but it just didn't seem to have any intensity to it. I really wanted to learn what it meant to follow Jesus with all of my heart, soul, mind and strength, but who would help me?

I attended a small youth conference in the fall of my second year in which an Italian guy named Luciano Del Monte was speaking. He was thirteen years my senior and was working on the university campus under the banner of the Navigators organization, a Christian campus group. I can't remember what he spoke about, yet something about him intrigued me. During one of the breaks, I sat across the table from him, looked straight at him and said, "You are going to mentor me." I wasn't going to give him an option – I was desperate to get guidance.

I had no idea the impact that was going to have on my life.

We met weekly for the next three years, in addition to attending the weekly Navigators meeting that he led. I learned about prayer, scripture meditation, spiritual disciplines and more. Most importantly, however, over and above my own spiritual growth and development, I learned the art of discipleship. The simple act of coming alongside a few other individuals to train them to be followers of Jesus and then to release them to do the same.

Since 1990, I have carried on with what I was taught by Luciano. I spent the first twelve years in the Canadian banking world working in downtown Toronto, Ontario, all the while finding guys to meet with for the purposes of discipleship.

In 2004, I began a whole new journey as a pastor in London, Ontario, Canada, at North Park Community Church. Although my responsibilities at the church have taken many forms over the years, at the core of what I have done is to come alongside a few other men to train them in the art of becoming a disciple and challenging them to do the same.

As the team of those who are discipling others at North Park has increased, I have taken on the role of encourager and guide. Some have even taken on the role of leading others without ever having experienced the joy of someone first coming alongside them. I applaud them for taking on the challenge.

In 2012, I graduated with a Doctor of Ministry at Tyndale Seminary in Toronto. My research focused on discipleship and the complexities that it entails. It further enhanced my understanding of life change and the importance of integrating many different activities for maximum life change.

Letters to Garret represents much of the teaching that I have been passing on over the past few years. Garret is not a specific individual, but rather represents a compilation of many of the people I've worked with and the ways in which I have been able to encourage them.

Read them in one sitting; read one a week and digest it; bounce around the book if you like. I think you'll find that you can keep coming back to them as you embrace the grand experience of discipling others.

I pray that these letters will encourage you as they have those I have had the privilege of coming alongside.

Matthew Eckert
London, Ontario, Canada

INTRODUCTION

It seems like every few years, a new fad sweeps through churches in North America. These have included Small Groups, Seeker Sensitive, Church Growth, Church Satellites, Church Planting, Missional movements, to name a few. Each promises great things and many pastors and church leaders jump from one to the next. Books are written, conferences are started, consultants prepare their presentations and promise great outcomes.

The term "discipleship" has come on stream in the last couple of years.

Organizations are putting out discipleship plans. Many promise great results. Move your people through this plan over six months or take them through this seminar and out comes a disciple of Jesus.

I am concerned that once again many pastors and church leaders will buy the programs, begin strong for a year or so and then slowly fade away as they don't see the results that they are promised or that they would like to see. Then it's off to the next program.

Many of us over the years have been committed to the hard work of what I'll refer to as "life-on-life discipleship." Although we are excited that the term has come in vogue, we are also aware that it won't take long until it too passes away into the void of other church ideas to make way for something else. I don't doubt the desire of any of these pastors; they truly do have a passion to see those in their local church to have a deep and rich faith in Jesus.

For some, many people have come into their churches recently, many returning after years away. These pastors have asked them to take on volunteer roles to help with weekend services. Many are shuffled into a small group and expected to grow – sometimes it works, often times it does not.

So what do they do? How do they manage the many pressures on them from their leadership boards and committees to make things happen in their church?

There are a few things that I believe must be understood at the outset when thinking about discipleship.

1. You can't program it. You can't move people through a program and expect committed followers of Jesus at the other end. Sure, there will be programmatic elements to it and curricula that you will probably use as well as gathering together on a consistent basis. However, at its core it is not a program.

2. It is highly relational. This involves vulnerability. This involves truly getting to know one another. This means that it can't be done in large groups to be effective, although gathering in a larger group may be a component of it.

3. It takes time; in my experience, at least two years of commitment to a person. As such, it can appear inefficient, laborious and even ineffective. Many aren't willing to put in the work.

4. Many won't want to commit. To be in an intentional long term commitment to grow deep in faith is not seen as exciting to many. Let's face it, in my experience, many (maybe most) church attenders do not want to be disciples of Jesus, to "seek God with all their heart, mind, and strength." They don't want to "deny themselves, take up their cross daily and follow." They don't want to "press on toward the goal to win the prize for which God has called them heavenward in Christ Jesus." This doesn't mean that you don't move forward with those who desire it, just don't expect many to line up or to really commit to the journey.

5. Pastors (and others who have thought about this) may not really believe that it is worth their time as they don't stick around long enough in one location to even attempt to make it a reality. It is my opinion that it would actually take six years of commitment to a discipling process to be convinced that it is worth your time, let alone asking others to make it part of their lives. First, you need to commit to building into the lives of two people for two years. Then, watch them move ahead as they themselves build into the lives of two people for two years. Finally, watch that next generation spend two years building into the lives of two others and see the impact that takes place beyond your direct influence. Only then will you be truly convinced to give your life to this. More on the specifics of two years and two people in a bit.

6. It's worth every amount of time and energy you give to it. I've been engaged in the ongoing process of guiding others for twenty-five years. To watch someone come alive as they encounter Jesus through the scriptures, prayer, service and deep relationships is fun beyond what you can describe. Then to see them go a do the same with others is absolutely incredible to watch.

In Matthew 28:18-20 we read about the marching orders that Jesus gave to his disciples as he left Earth. "Go and make disciples..." were his words. In simple terms, we know that a disciple of Jesus is a learner of Jesus, one who wants to follow His ways. I don't think that I would get much objection to this from pastors and church leaders. The vast majority of pastors and church leaders would completely agree that we are called to make disciples. The question has really never been what, the conversation is always around the HOW. How are we to make disciples? Not only that, but HOW do we do it in our present cultural context? For Jesus, his disciples were actually with him continuously. You obviously won't do that in the twenty-first century.

Now, let me be clear. I fully believe that there are many activities that speak into the life of a Christian that guide them on a journey to being a disciple of Jesus, and that, in reality, no one ever fully arrives at being a "completed" disciple this side of Heaven. In reality, if you are on the journey, then you have arrived. I like to say that the journey is the destination. If you are continually progressing then you have arrived. The sad reality is that, in many cases, Christians attending weekend services have stagnated, they have stopped progressing, their journey has been sidelined, and as such, I would argue that they have ceased to be a disciple of Jesus. This is harsh perhaps, but it is my opinion. Please note that this isn't a question about whether or not they are a Christian, it is a question about whether as a Christian they are a disciple. Can you have one without the other? I would suggest that you can. Let the theological conversation begin, just not in this book.

Please understand that I am a big proponent of local church involvement. This includes attending a weekly service, serving in an area of your local church, and perhaps being part of a small group. In addition, I believe that we are called to live beyond ourselves and our own local church context to serve our local community and engage with those who have been sidelined by our culture. All of these activities are components of a mature Christian.

Beyond these activities, I am a strong proponent of what I'll refer to as life-on-life discipleship. This is to intentionally come alongside others and guide them on their journey of faith with the express outcome that they will know how to feed themselves spiritually and that they will then come alongside others in the same intentional way. The other components will continue to be a part of their life of faith, perhaps even in the context of the life-on-life discipling relationship. In no way do I believe that this relational engagement is done as an independent component void of an active local church commitment, and may it never be.

My ongoing desire is to continue to raise up a generation of individuals that will commit themselves to intentionally walking alongside others.

My personal experience, and what I will be articulating in these letters, has been that this is best done in groups of three – one leader and two learners; I refer to these as triads. I also believe that this is very doable in our North American cultural context.

Here is my rationale for three people:

1. You can't hide in a group of three. If you commit, you will need to participate.

2. It is easier to schedule. If your regular time to meet one week gets disrupted due to someone's schedule, you can typically find another time to meet without disrupting the flow.

3. Many more people will feel confident to lead a group of this size.

4. It provides better conversation than a one-on-one mentoring relationship, which feels more hierarchical.

Practically speaking, here is what my discipleship commitment looks like for those that I come alongside.

1. I commit to meeting with two guys for two years – they know this up front. Sometimes they know each other before we begin, often times they do not.

2. I tell them that I expect them to be willing to commit to coming alongside others when we are finished our two years together, and trusting that they will make this part of their life work; to consider this work of life-on-life discipleship as one of their ongoing spiritual disciplines.

3. We meet on a weekly basis for up to two hours. I strongly believe that unless you meet weekly, you will lose momentum. Every other week just doesn't work, in my opinion. I believe that this can work in our North American cultural context.

4. Our weekly meeting involves working through a curriculum that includes pre-work as well as scripture memory. You can

read some of the letters that outline my thinking about curriculum. In reality, many people have never established any personal rhythms of reading the Bible and reflecting on it. It is critical that they begin this as part of our journey. Remember, I am helping them to learn how to feed themselves spiritually.

5. Beyond our weekly get-together, I find a place for us to serve together. This may include one-off opportunities or consistent times. For me, this has included serving breakfast at one of our city's homeless shelters, constructing items for non-profits, serving together on a non-profit board and serving in our church's events together. These serving times reveal a lot about our personalities and are invaluable to our ongoing relational development.

6. I bring them together for an annual retreat. This includes not only the guys I'm meeting with, but others who are connected to a triad. Amazing things happen on these retreats and I am able to reinforce the vision of life-on-life discipleship to everyone there. Amazingly, one man who has been with me for a while has now ventured out on his own and is planning his own retreat with guys that he has been building into over the past few years. An entirely new base has been established.

Beyond my own life-on-life discipling relationships, I have increased my intentionality of helping others as they have committed their lives to this. It has been fun to live vicariously through them as they impact the lives of others.

The letters in this book are mostly responses to questions that I have encountered when talking with them. These conversations have been energizing for me as they continually cause me to better articulate why I do what I do and how I do it.

I trust that these letters will help to sharpen your abilities. May they challenge you as well as encourage you. May they help you to better articulate why you would choose to engage in this lifestyle.

They don't need to be read in any particular order, although perhaps a quick read through to help orient yourself may be in order and then read the ones that will help you when the need arises. If there are others that are with you on this journey, I encourage you to read and discuss them together. Try to articulate why you agree with the letter, or why you don't.

Beyond this book, I encourage you to simply get out there and begin to build into two lives. The best way to understand these letters is to be in the trenches and involved in the practical day-to-day involvement in life-on-life discipleship. The purpose of this book is to practically help with the question of how we make disciples in our cultural context, as Jesus has called us to.

One final note. In these letters, I often refer to the "guys" that I am coming alongside as my work is with men. I do not recommend discipling relationships between genders unless of course it is your spouse or children. Even then, it is probably best that they have another voice speaking into their lives, since they are so close to you and probably live with you. The thoughts presented in these letters is not specific to men; they are valid for both men and women. In fact, some of the letters were inspired from conversations with my wife, who is consistently deeply invested in the lives of two women. If you are a woman reading this, you can simply replace "guys" with "gals" as you read.

Blessings as you engage with these letters. May you find wind in your sails as you involve yourself in this beautiful work of life-on-life discipleship.

For the Kingdom of God.

Matthew Eckert
London, Ontario, Canada
www.mattheweckert.com

ACKNOWLEDGEMENTS

Who do you acknowledge when writing your first book? It is a fascinating thing to contemplate.

My wife, Janice, has always been a huge encourager in my life. She is also in the trenches with me as she comes alongside other women in the same way. It is always great to compare notes on what we learn about the process and how lives change. She also has an uncanny ability to see into someone's heart and know when they need to be encouraged instead of challenged; I have much to learn from her.

My parents, John and Viola Eckert. Although they live two hours' drive away, they are always boosting my confidence. They have read every letter in this book and provided their thoughts. Even in their early eighties and late seventies, they continue to serve in their local church and weekly bring together a small group of people to learn together and pray for each other.

For mentors in my life who have modelled this so well, including Luciano and Rosetta Del Monte, Paul and Phyllis Stanley, Peter and Cathy Kuehni. They are relentless in their commitment to come alongside others without recognition or fanfare. They have done this for decades and will continue to until God takes them from this world. I am privileged to be associated with all of you.

To the many guys that have allowed me into their lives over the past twenty-five years. They have allowed me to encourage them, to challenge them, to mourn with them and to rejoice with them.

To the church where I am a pastor, North Park Community Church. They have given me a lot of freedom over the past ten years to experiment with ways to help people become disciples of Jesus.

Finally, to anyone who has chosen to be in the trenches to intentionally build into the lives of others. You are an amazing group of people. I applaud your efforts and commitment.

LETTER OF INTRODUCTION

Dear Garret,

It sure was a great two years that we were able to meet so regularly for the purpose of growing in our faith. You allowed me to lead you during this time and I want you to know that I don't take this privilege lightly. You had a very teachable spirit and a deep passion to grow. I appreciated your commitment to the discipling process; you made getting together such a joy. You were always engaged and took it so seriously. We laughed a lot, challenged each other in so many ways, and grew in our love of God and others.

Your love of scripture was so evident, especially how you always wanted to make it relevant to your life in your family and work situations. Scripture memory was always engaging and I believe that we were able to plumb the depths of the verses in amazing ways as we meditated on them in the group and tossed around the words and phrases.

I appreciated the depth and passion of your prayers; I learned a lot listening to you pray. It was never shallow and hurried. Prayer was very meaningful to you as you wrestled to find the words that best portrayed what your wanted to tell God. You modelled this well for me and I will always be grateful.

We were able to serve together as well. I remember building those picnic tables for a non-profit organization during that early snow storm one December. By the time we were done, we almost couldn't get our cars out of the parking lot. It was great having our kids there with us as well. In addition, we regularly served breakfast at the Crash Beds downtown at 6:30. I'm not sure we have any greater understanding of the issues surrounding homelessness, however I believe that we were a small part of the solution.

I enjoyed many great conversations at our favourite restaurant, eating peanuts and nachos late into the night (I'm sorry your football team continues to suffer). I recall the many drawings we created on napkins as we wrestled with issues of faith and discipleship and how to engage our church in deeper ways. I'm not sure we answered all of our questions, but it did sharpen our thinking. I remember reviewing our memory verses and thinking about how they impacted our lives – we often wondered what those around us would think of our conversations, but we didn't care. This was life-giving for us.

Now this stage of our journey is done. I've taught you what I could. Although not perfect, I've modelled what I know to this stage of my journey of faith. I know that I'll continue to grow and develop and hopefully the next couple of guys I give two years to will benefit from what I've learned from us getting together. We never stop developing and yet we can't let our lack of perfection stop us from helping others. With God's help, we can give to others.

It is time for you to move on and take what you've learned from me, blend it with your own unique personality and style, and come alongside some other guys. You have a lot to offer and I know that you will be an amazing influence.

Please understand that this is by no means goodbye. We will always be friends and will continue to connect. I want to move into a role of mentor as you embrace your own questions of leadership. No doubt you will have many questions. Send them my way and I'll respond as I am able.

I'm very much looking forward to this next stage of our relationship and excited to see how you will be used by God in the lives of others.

Blessings for the future.
Matthew

FEAR

Dear Garret,

    The question of fear always comes up when we choose to take responsibility for someone else's growth. You asked if this sense of fear will ever go away, especially as you embark on this journey of leadership yourself.

    I recall reading a quotation from the great tenor Luciano Pavarotti. He said, "Am I afraid of high notes? Of course I am afraid. What sane man is not?"

    I think that it's important to address the topic of fear when it comes to leading others in a life-on-life discipling relationship. Just to be clear, after twenty-five years of personal involvement, I can honestly say that I still have fear; I still question many things. Let me share a few of my fears. Perhaps they are yours as well.

    1) Will the guys like me? It might sound strange to begin with this, but I guess I'm human; we all want to be liked. In leading others through a process of learning what it means to be a disciple of Jesus, I'm going to touch on topics that will be challenging. I'm going to ask them to do things that they might not really want to do (think scripture memory) or they might think strange. They will also see parts of my personality that will probably be different from what they are expecting. I'm afraid that they might think less

of me or think bad thoughts of me or think I don't know what I'm doing. I fear this.

2) Does the discipling process I engage in work? From a human perspective, I can only see the external impact, what a person is now doing as a result of meeting with me (scripture reading and study, prayer, service to others, etc.), I can never see the heart. Are the guys I meet with only going through the motions? Am I wasting my time? Once we have finished connecting, typically for up to two years, will they have caught the vision for discipleship or has the time resulted in very little life change? Is fear too strong a word to use here? Perhaps, but I do fear that my approach may not always be effective.

3) Will we like each other? Many of the guys I connect with have never met each other before we begin our journey together. In asking guys to join with me, I try to be sensitive to their personalities and life stages so that there is a better chance of us starting off strong. But will we? Interestingly, I don't think Jesus worried about this when you look at the cross section of people that he chose to build into. In fact, it's amazing that they were able to stay together for three years without physically hurting each other! I want us as a group to develop an intimacy of friendship, that we can trust each other, that we like being together. I fear this won't be the case.

4) Do I have what it takes? After all, who do I think I am, taking responsibility for the spiritual growth and development of other men? Am I really qualified? Will I have ALL of the answers to their questions (the answer is no)? In reflecting on all the guys that I have met with over the years, I still fear that I may not have the skills to help someone learn what it means to be a disciple of Jesus. This is especially true when I am leading people that are older than I am. I can recall times in my mid-thirties when I was coming alongside guys in their fifties who had grown up in the church. They had led at varying levels in their churches and yet no one had ever come alongside them to help them understand what following Jesus meant (fascinating to think that someone could

be a key leader in a church and not truly understand and live out what being a disciple of Jesus is). I often felt inadequate thinking that perhaps they should be leading me, and yet they chose to allow me to lead them. I am honoured at their trust in me, and yet I feared that I had what it takes.

Perhaps you are having some of these fears. Perhaps you have some of your own. Fear can be prolific and it will grow in very unreasonable ways if we let it.

However, in all of these fears, I've become convinced that I am called to simply enter into these relationships out of a sense of obedience. I look around at what I see as "bored Christians", who are going through the weekend church routine without truly engaging their faith, and I think, "Someone needs to do this. If not I, then who?"

If you think about it, we all want to be liked, and yet we won't always be. We all wonder if lives are really being changed, and yet we've witnessed enough amazing life changing stories to know the Holy Spirit is still actively working. Look at your own life. We all want to be part of the perfect community where everyone gets along, and yet the only way to get there is to model it to others and enter into the hard work of making relationships work. Finally, none of us has what it takes, and yet Jesus still calls us to this work.

In this we can agree with the Apostle Paul in 2 Corinthians: "But he [Jesus] said to me, 'My grace is sufficient for you, for my power is made perfect in weakness.' Therefore, I will boast all the more gladly about my weaknesses, so that Christ's power may rest on me. That is why, for Christ's sake, I delight in weaknesses, in insults, in hardships, in persecutions, in difficulties. For when I am weak, then I am strong."

May you sense the power of the Holy Spirit in your life to overcome your fears as you engage in the wonderful work of helping others become disciples of Jesus.

Matthew

IT'S ALL ABOUT TIME

Dear Garret,

As we've discussed on many occasions, we are both always intrigued with how people choose to spend their time. Many people we know claim to be followers of Jesus, and yet when we look at how they spend their time, we have to wonder what priority he really has in their lives. Part of our role as disciple makers is to help people understand how their time is a resource and how they allocate it reflects their love for Jesus.

I know for me, time is on my mind whenever I begin with a new group of guys. In fact, even as I drive to meet my new group for the discipleship meetings, I can't help but think to myself, "Here we go again."

Each group of guys replaces the discipleship group that I just finished connecting with and who would have been with me for almost two years – you were part of my last group. I've given them what I believe they need to take the next step.

Whether they like it or not—and whether I like it or not—they don't need me anymore, and I do them no favours by continuing to meet with them on a weekly basis to study and pray as well as to serve together. It's time for them to move on. Sink or swim.

As life-on-life disciple-makers, we always have time on our minds. The clock is always ticking, each day, each week, each month, and each year. We try to maximize it all. We get no more or no less than anyone else does. Before us are a couple of guys that have decided to trust their lives to us. It's all about time.

My Time: As the leader of the group, I recognize that I have committed my time. Time to review the weekly material that we will work through. Time to review the memory verses that we'll engage with. Time to think about and pray for these guys that I believe God wants to do some amazing work in. Time to get up at 5:15am to be able to start our 6:00 a.m. gathering (I know that you are more an evening guy, so for you it's 8:00 p.m.). Time to call them between gatherings to check in, send them cards of encouragement, and invite them over from time to time. I have chosen to say yes to them, which means that I have chosen to say no to something or someone else. I only have so much time, and every "yes" also means "no".

Development Time: There are no quick roads to discipleship, as you very well know. It takes a couple of years for someone to be at a point where they have embraced the important and life-giving habits in their walk with God. That they in essence have learned to feed themselves spiritually and are ready to venture out and take responsibility to build into the lives of others. This won't happen in a weekend seminar or a message on Sunday – although these activities may create the momentum to desire something deeper. I recognize that over the next couple of years, the guys I meet with will be encouraged one week and frustrated the next. They'll be enamoured with who God is one week and mad at him the next. They'll be ready to take on the world one week and question their faith the next. It's all part of the journey that I will get to experience with them. It won't happen in a day; it takes time.

The Ending Time: I must always begin the journey in discipling others with the end in mind. There will come a day when I must move on, for all of our sakes. It would be very easy to simply stay with the same group of guys for decades and find a comfortable place to connect. Yet life isn't about my comfort, it's about the Kingdom of God. It has also been my experience that any group that meets for too long eventually loses its edge and becomes lethargic. In the process of discipleship, one cannot always stay as the learner; you must become the teacher.

So as you begin your journey of building into the lives of others, remember, it's all about TIME.

Matthew

CONVERSATIONS

Dear Garret,

As you engage in the discipling process, take note of the conversations that are taking place. Over the years, I've discovered a couple of different types of conversations that are a distraction and that seldom lead to any life change. It is important that you address these for the benefit of everyone, especially early in the process.

1) "They" Syndrome People – These are people who talk about the world at large. They talk about how "people" do this or that, and can't seem to or don't want to make it applicable for themselves. If you are talking about sin, they might say that "people don't want to admit when they are wrong" or "I have an uncle who…". Seldom can they look at themselves and name a sin that they struggle with.

If you are talking about the importance of scripture, they might say that "it is important that people read and study the Bible," and "the church should use the Bible more during services," but won't talk about the practicalities of their own experience reading scripture and what they need to do next in order to make it a reality in their lives.

Unless there is applicability for someone's life that they can articulate, there can't be life change. Talking about someone else may be okay in certain aspects of life, but when it comes to being a disciple of Jesus, it needs to get very personal. Each person must see how it applies to them directly so that as they go about their day, it can be applied for them. As Jesus said in Matthew 7, I need to "take the plank out of my own eye, and then I'll see clearly to remove the speck from my brother's eye."

2) Off Topic People – These people always have another conversation they want to engage in, and it is seldom the topic on the agenda. At times it seems as though they feel smart by bringing up other questions that they are thinking about or that they heard someone else engaging in. Yet, as the leader, you are taking people on a journey of growth, and constantly being distracted by random questions will never fulfill the greater purpose.

In no way am I saying to ignore the questions that people have about life issues they are working through, yet perhaps these questions will get answered over time as they enter into the discipling relationship. I've found that the off topic questions people ask are seldom that pressing that they can't wait for them to be answered. Often times, as their relationship with Jesus grows, these questions become less important and often irrelevant. Honestly, continually taking rabbit trails based on the whims of someone's questions seldom leads to long term growth.

My father tells the story of a friend he went to Bible school with. This friend always had another agenda. When the class was studying Ephesians, his friend spent his time studying Isaiah; when the class looked at church history, he was distracted by apologetics. Needless to say, he never did graduate and has never gained any traction in life.

At some point, those you are leading will need to trust you and the journey you are taking them on. If they have another agenda to pursue, perhaps connecting with you isn't the right thing for them.

Matthew

LEAD, DON'T FACILITATE

Dear Garret,

I'm excited to hear about the traction that you are making with the guys you've begun to meet with. It looks like you haven't missed a beat since you went on your own and chose to build into the lives of two others.

I want to caution you in the area of leading versus facilitating – it can be a slippery slope that I think you need to be wary of.

I'm continually fascinated with the word "facilitate" that is consistently used in many group settings I've come across, especially in churches. "Small Groups" have people who *facilitate* discussions. People attend meetings to make decisions that are *facilitated* by one of the members.

At the core of this is perhaps a desire to demonstrate that we are all equal partners, that no one person is better than the other, that everyone's ideas are good ideas and need to be listened to and respected and that somehow the group will come to the best and most reliable conclusion through facilitation.

When it comes to discipleship, let's declare the idea of facilitation not as progressive and meaningful but as misguided and counterproductive.

When you begin the journey to help others become disciples of Jesus, either you asked someone to join you or someone came to you. In either case, these individuals assume that you are further down the road of being a disciple of Jesus than they are and that you have something to offer them that they sense is missing in their lives. Whether you like it or not, they are looking to you to take them somewhere and it is time for you to step up and lead, not facilitate. You are the one guiding the discussion, you are the one asking them to engage in spiritual disciplines that they have never or seldom engaged in and you are the one sharing your life journey as something to imitate. We are not perfect and we continue to learn, yet with the confidence of the Apostle Paul we need to step out and say "Imitate me" (1 Corinthians 4:16).

Without a leader, groups grow stale and naturally die out. Let's stop thinking that being nice by facilitating is the most Christian way to pursue discipleship. It is not. It has been my experience that people want to be led. Interestingly, even though I lead others on the journey of discipleship, I still look to others with more experience to lead me and you need to do the same. You have never fully arrived, we are always on a journey of becoming more like Jesus.

I ask you to lead confidently with the belief that you are called to engage others in true discipleship. Those you lead will be better off and thank you for it.

Matthew

SCRIPTURE MEMORY

Dear Garret,

As usual, the topic of scripture memory will come up. It is one of those areas that I am so often challenged on. So many excuses are used as to why people don't want to engage in this and yet, as we experienced, it is so life-giving. It is amazing how often these verses will come to mind during our days, just when we need them.

Dallas Willard wrote the following: *"The primary freedom we have is always the choice of where we will place our minds... To that end [scripture] memorization is vital. It is astonishing how little of the Bible is known 'by heart' by people who profess to honor it. If we do not know it how can it help us? It cannot. Memorization, by contrast, enables us to keep it constantly before our minds."* Dallas Willard (www.dwillard.org/articles)

You may recall the incident I shared with you when we met. A number of years ago, I was in a meeting at which a Christian psychiatrist was asked to share about how to assist those who live with various mental issues. Although the content was interesting, what he shared about himself personally was the most impacting on my life. He mentioned that he consistently memorized entire chapters of scripture for his own mental health. He had my attention.

He talked about research on the brain and how what we decide to allow in over time creates what he referred to as roads. The more we allow certain content in, the wider this road becomes, at times becoming a multi-lane highway, allowing this information to flow freely. It was his intent to create highways of scripture in his mind, and the only way for this to happen was for him to memorize entire chapters of scripture.

From my reading of history, it is my understanding that by the age of eight years old, Jewish children had memorized the first five books of the Bible. Some went on to memorize the rest of what we refer to as the OT by the age of thirteen. As such, Jesus and his disciples would have had our entire OT memorized! Apparently, this still goes on today in some Jewish Synagogues. I can't confirm this, but is definitely makes you think.

You know me well enough to understand that I will always be a big proponent of scripture memory. However, if there is one thing that I get the most push-back from in the discipleship process, it is the aspect of memorizing scripture: "I can't memorize," "it's too difficult," "I'll just read it over many times and I'll get the point." No, no, and no.

Let's reiterate this once again: discipleship is not easy. Discipleship is not a side-hobby. To be a disciple is to make it your life. This is not something we play with when convenient, it is who we are.

And I can think of no better way for our standard learning textbook, the Bible, to make a lasting impact on our lives than to memorize it, and then to recite it over and over, allowing the words and the phrases to seep into every aspect of who we are, to guide our prayers, to influence our relationships and to help us make life decisions.

As one who leads others on the road of discipleship, it is your job to set the pace. I encourage you that the discipline of memorization, once engaged in for a period of time, will become so meaningful, so life-changing, that you may not even use the word "discipline" to describe it anymore. It will become a craving, although I don't think I really need to tell you this as you are already fully convinced.

Of all the guys that I have spent time with in a discipling relationship over the years, the one aspect that keeps coming up as the most beneficial is the aspect of scripture memorization. They start the journey simply doing it because I ask them to, and along the journey they thank me for sticking with it.

You will need to develop your own convictions on this. You will also need to develop your own ways of encouraging those that you lead to engage in it.

Be confident. Memorization should not be seen as an optional "nice to have" aspect of the disciple, it is foundational. We will all develop highways of learning in our minds that will influence our actions, the question is, which ones?

Matthew

STAY FOCUSED

Dear Garret,

What is the purpose of a discipling relationship? What are you trying to accomplish? What topics should be discussed? What should be the focus of the training and the conversation?

A mentor of mine would always say to me, "People have felt needs and they have unfelt needs. Acknowledge the felt needs, but make sure you don't forget the unfelt needs."

Far too often I see groups gathering together to focus on their felt needs. They want to discuss the latest book that's covering a trendy topic or listen to the latest DVD from a favourite speaker who stirs up their passion and emotions. They want to discuss issues relating to their marriage or parenting or finances. All of these things may be good at certain times and have their place. You will even incorporate some aspects of these in the discipling process. But I want to argue that this is not the core of a discipling relationship. This is not your purpose or focus if your desire to lead others in the path of discipleship.

I think you will notice that as a person matures in their faith in Jesus, they naturally gravitate to church programs less and less because they have figured out how to feed themselves spiritually. They don't chase after trendy topics or the latest seminar, because they are being fed in the daily, weekly, monthly and yearly disciplines that they have developed for themselves and their spiritual health. As a result of these disciplines, they naturally know how to draw on the necessary resources to ensure strong relationships, to have financial integrity and to maintain a strong faith regardless of what life throws at them.

This is your role as a disciple-maker. You are helping others to develop life disciplines, habits and routines that will enable them to have the wherewithal to know what it takes to sustain themselves. They will know that they need regular biblical input, and they will do it. They will know that they need regular times of prayer, both by themselves and with others, and they will do it. They will know that they can't do life alone, that they need others around them, and they will do it. They will know they have God-given gifts to serve the church and their community for the sake of the Kingdom of God, and they will do it. They will know that the Holy Spirit can and will speak to them in unique ways, and they will listen.

They won't need prodding, coaxing or cajoling. They won't need to be revved up every week at a church service to gas them up for the next seven days. They won't need to find trendy topics and conversations to engage in.

They will be disciples. They will be followers of Jesus. You will become less important in their lives, Jesus will become more important. That is your focus; that is your purpose. Don't let anyone allow you to get off track with the latest and the greatest. Develop disciples. Period.

Matthew

OBEDIENCE TO THE PROCESS

Dear Garret,

There is an insidious side to discipleship that we need to watch out for or it will discourage our efforts and cause us to want to quit.

In every discipling relationship I engage in, I desperately want to witness life change—preferably something significant. Each time I meet with the guys I'm connecting with, I look for every sign of positive growth. Is the conversation deeper than the last time we met? Do their prayers sound more passionate? Are they enjoying scripture more? Are they intentionally engaged in acts of service?

When I see what I deem as growth, inwardly I celebrate and at times pat myself on the back. When I don't see what I deem as growth, I might get frustrated and discouraged. Often times it even leads me to long periods of prayer telling God what he needs to be doing on my behalf so that I'll see the growth that I want to see.

STOP!

Why this desire on my part to see growth? Why do I think that I know what growth even looks like?

I recall a situation in which someone I had met with was moving out of the city. We had connected for about a year and I honestly felt that the life change I was hoping for never materialized, and now he was leaving. I chalked it up to a good but not significant experience and moved on. Six months after he left, he called me. He thanked me for the huge impact that I had had on his life and that he had already rallied a few guys around him for the purposes of helping them grow as disciples, and he was leading the group!

That was five years ago. To this day he continues to intentionally build into the lives of others. He loves God passionately, engages with scripture regularly, and leads his family and business with integrity. He has every reason available as to why he is too busy to seek out other guys to lead. Yet something profound happened to him in our time together. I didn't witness it when I wanted to, and yet God was doing an amazing work in his life.

We have chosen to intentionally build into the lives of others. To go the distance. Life-on-life. Long-haul stuff. Yet in the course of each relationship, we need to continually remind ourselves that we are simply called to be obedient to each relationship. Whether someone gets it in the end is not our decision or responsibility. We cannot live for the accolades of others. We need only live for the affirmation of Jesus: "Well done, good and faithful servant."

Jesus said, "All authority in Heaven and on Earth has been given to me, therefore go and make disciples…" Matthew 28:18-20. The authority is Jesus', mine is making disciples. Jesus causes the life change, we are simply the instrument he uses. We need to relax and just do what we are called to do. Life change is not our responsibility. "My yoke is easy and my burden is light" Jesus said. That's the life I want to live. I believe that this is also what you desire. Stay faithful. Stick to the course.

Over the years, it you choose to stay faithful to this process, you will no doubt encounter those who you truly doubt are growing and it may discourage you. They may appear anemic or uninterested or perhaps you believe that you never had the necessary time to complete the process. May I encourage you to simply do what you believe you were called to do with the time you have been given. God will work in ways that we can never fathom.

"Well done, good and faithful servant" is all I want to hear.

Matthew

CURRICULUM

Dear Garret,

  Thanks for your question about curriculum. It is important for you to establish the material that you will use in your discipling process. You know that I believe in the importance of some type of formal material to guide the learning, otherwise the conversation will be random with no apparent learning taking place. I recognize that learning styles vary and thus you will need to be sensitive to this. However, I strongly believe that you need to have something specific that you will use.

  Did you ever wonder why most curriculum that is developed for spiritual growth (i.e. church small group material) is typically 6-8 weeks in length? Ever wonder why the majority of curriculum embraced by churches is DVD based requiring no preparation for both the attendee and the leader?

  Although I have not researched this specifically, my experience would tell me that there are two reasons: novelty and effort (or lack of). We continually demand new stimuli and we don't want to work at it.

  Discipleship does not embrace this. Yet you do need curriculum, something to take you where you want to go. You can make up your own or use something that already exists. Though there have been many curriculum options developed over the years, not all are created equal.

Since 2004, I have chosen a book called *Discipleship Essentials* by Greg Ogden, a twenty-five session model that establishes the foundations for the disciple. You will recall that we worked through this material when we first met. I have worked through this book a number of times with different guys.

You might ask, don't I get bored with it? Not at all. In fact, with each group I take through it, new questions come up and I see the material in new ways. Remember, my goal is to help people become disciples, to establish the basics in their lives, not to read the latest and greatest book.

Apart from the topics covered, why do I believe this curriculum is effective?

First, twenty-five weeks allows for habits to actually be formed. Most groups of guys I meet with will typically "hit the wall" around weeks 6-8, the usual length of most curriculum developed. After this time the novelty wears off and we move into the zone of true discipline. Each member has to ask themselves, am I in or not? You can liken this to any type of physical exercise regimen. Many people begin their membership in January, and by the end of February they've stopped, unwilling to do the hard work and as a result they never see the benefits.

Second, there is pre-work. At the very least, if a guy spends 15-20 minutes a day for four days of the week, they can accomplish the work. For most, even this little amount of investment in their relationship with God is a huge step, yet it is necessary. It is always exciting to see how, over time, many of the guys will go beyond the assigned work and begin to dig into other scriptures and readings that enhance their learning.

Third, scripture memory. I have already commented on this in a previous writing. Suffice it to say that this aspect must always be part of the discipling process. No questions. By the end of the particular curriculum that I have chosen to use, they will have memorized more than twenty-five sets of verses, and they always comment on the significant impact it has had on them personally and relationally. I wouldn't have it any other way. Avoid including scripture memory at your peril.

There are other items I might insert from time to time into the process and other curriculum ideas that I use once this initial twenty-five session unit is completed, but I've chosen this to form the foundation. Interestingly, what I have also found is that once we've established some healthy patterns, everything else we do takes on a new energy, the guys just know what to do.

One person I've met with for a while is reading through the Bible and simply wants to dialogue about what he is learning. He has developed the necessary habits, is self-motivated, and we can embrace the Bible together each week. He also has his own group of guys that he is developing and will be a great living example with the habits that he has developed.

Find the curriculum that works for you, ensure that it develops the habits of a disciple, and move forward. However, don't ever settle for mediocrity. Push through the novelty barriers and enjoy the fruit that comes from embracing the richness of discipleship.

Matthew

IT'S ALL ABOUT LOVE

Dear Garret,

With all the talk about disciplines and meeting and commitment to the discipling process, it can feel like a regimented boot camp process that you are driving guys through. Let me comment on this.

The Apostle Paul wrote the following: "We weren't aloof with you. We took you just as you were. We were never patronizing, never condescending, but *we cared for you* the way a mother cares for her children. *We loved you dearly.* Not content to just pass on the Message, we wanted to *give you our hearts.* And we did" 1 Thessalonians 2:7-8 (Message).

If there is one thing that separates a mediocre discipling experience from a life changing one, it is love from the leader. That's you. You must fully embrace those that you are leading. You need to pour out your life into theirs with a love that goes far beyond any feeling or emotion. You must love those you lead when they energize you and when they frustrate you, when they take initiative and when they don't want to even show up, let alone complete any assignment you have given. You need to love them when they ask questions that you think are meaningless and simply a distraction. You must love them so much that you can't wait to see them again just to hear about their week, the little things and the big. You must love them so that you pray for them as though praying for your own children.

"*He had loved his disciples* during his ministry on Earth, and now *he loved them to the very end*…. Then he began to wash the disciples' feet…" John 13

These words from the Gospel of John always cut me to the core. Interestingly, during this foot washing episode, the disciples still didn't understand what was happening, yet Jesus continued on. I often wonder how frustrated Jesus was with his disciples. He even washed the feet of Judas who was about to betray him.

The journey of discipleship is so much more than a program you take someone through, it is more than a linear process full of activities that get checked off. Discipleship is you. It is you giving yourself to someone else. It will keep you up at night when you don't believe that those you are building into really want to commit, to "deny themselves and take up their cross." You will feel the pain when their relational world is in turmoil and they question everything.

It is also exuberance when the light turns on and the scriptures come alive to them. It is gratitude for having been able to share the deepest aspects of life together knowing that it is a safe place for all of you.

Let's agree with John. "Dear friends, I am not writing a new commandment for you; rather it is an old one you have had from the very beginning. This old commandment—to *love one another*—is the same message you heard before. Yet it is also new. *Jesus lived the truth of this commandment*, and you also are living it" (1 John 2:7-8).

Love those that you lead. There really is no other way.

Matthew

QUESTIONS

Dear Garret,

It was fun hanging out last night reflecting on what you have been learning as you are leading the two guys in your group. As we dialogued, it became apparent how important our ability to ask good questions is. They are at the heart of any vibrant discipling relationship. A good question will move someone beyond simple information gathering to life change.

Jesus spent much of his teaching in question mode. When he finished the story that we call "The Good Samaritan", he asked, "Who do you think the neighbour was?" When the disciples were with him on a boat during a storm, Jesus asked, "Why are you afraid?" The Pharisees challenged him about picking grain on the Sabbath, and Jesus asked them, "If you had one sheep, and it fell into a well on the Sabbath, wouldn't you get to work and pull it out?" At one point, alone with his disciples, Jesus asked, "Who do people say that the Son of Man is?" and then, "Who do you say I am?"

Over the years, I have experimented with a number of questions to help those I am leading to get to the point to life change. I want questions that will get them thinking deeply, at times I want to throw them off balance, to ask them something they aren't expecting. Although many questions will be topic specific, there are some that I've found work in many situations.

One that I've used often and continue to use is this: "If you really believed this, how would you live differently?" In asking this question, I like to emphasize the word "really". Saying it only once may not have the desired effect. This question moves people away from theoretical abstraction to on the ground, in your face, reality.

Take for example a conversation about sin. "For all have sinned and fall short of the glory of God" Romans 3:23. "For the wages of sin is death, but the gift of God is eternal life in Christ Jesus our Lord" Romans 6:23. "We all like sheep have gone astray, each of us has turned to our own way" Isaiah 53:6. "Surely I was sinful at birth, sinful from the time my mother conceived me" Psalm 51:5.

Many of the guys I've met with, if they were honest, actually think that they are okay. Sure they've done some bad things, but compared to others, they're pretty good.

There may be points in time in our lives that we feel sinful, yet more often than not, we don't. So, if I really, really, really, believed these verses, that I am a sinner, that I do fall short of God's glory, how would I live differently? How would my desire to serve God change? How would I treat others, knowing that none of us makes the grade?

In addition, I love to ask guys how they would parent differently. Do they see their children as sinful from birth? To be honest, most people truly think that their kids are born good and that somehow society makes them bad. Yet, if I truly believed these verses, it changes everything. I have to mold my kids from a standpoint of "born a sinner", versus a "protect them from other sinners in society" standpoint. Some guys don't want to hear that.

A well worded question changes the conversation. Continue to learn the power of the question. Develop your own arsenal, and watch the life change take place.

Matthew

PRAYER

Dear Garret,

As we so often have discussed, the aspect of prayer in the life of the disciple is so important to develop. It needs to become a central aspect of their life, but most importantly, it must be a key part of your life for those that you lead.

We must always realize that prayer is a discipline. I use the word discipline intentionally here because for many people it isn't a discipline at all; it is a life jacket or perhaps a bubble gum machine. It is a life jacket since it is only used when desperation sets in, we are drowning and we need God to save us. It is a bubble gum machine since we come to God with our to-do list that we want him to complete; we put in our quarter and expect the gum ball answers to come out.

Take some time to listen to people's prayers, or perhaps your own. What do you hear? As I've observed people's prayers over time and evaluated mine, I've noticed that they are quite selfish. God, give me this; God, I need that; God, help me accomplish stuff. We don't use those words per se, but at the heart of it our prayers are all about us. If we don't get it, we give up and wonder where God is.

In the call to make disciples, one of the disciplines we need to instill in those we are working with is a proper understanding of prayer. First and foremost, however, is our call to pray for those we lead. What we do and what we truly believe will always leak out. How you pray or don't pray, will be revealed.

In his book, *Shaped by the Word*, Robert Mulholland Jr. makes the following statement about disciplines: "Let me give you a litmus test to determine if you are engaging in a spiritual discipline. Are you willing to offer something to God as a discipline and to keep offering it day after day, week after week, month after month, year after year – to continue offering it for God to use in whatever way God wants in your life and *have God do absolutely nothing with it*? If you are, then you are engaging in a spiritual discipline that will cut to the heart of all of those debilitating dynamics of our culture and the false self it generates that tend to misshape our formation."

As one who is leading someone else on the journey of discipleship, you need to be on your knees in prayer for them. You must passionately call out to God on their behalf, for their growth and development, for their relationships, for the scriptures to come alive for them, for them to "deny themselves, take up their cross daily and follow." You must pray consistently, week after week, month after month, whether you see any growth or not. You must pray. The results are not your concern, only the action of prayer for them. As you do this, you will find yourself loving them more, wanting them to grow more, and caring for them more.

Do not stop engaging in the discipline of prayer. It is of utmost importance.

Matthew

RHYTHMS

Dear Garret,

One of the key changes that must take place as you begin to lead others on the journey of discipleship is the recognition of the importance of rhythms. When you are being led on this journey, your leader or guide will hold you accountable for your rhythms, asking about your prayers, scriptural input, and other disciplines. However, as you begin to lead others, you won't always have someone asking you these questions, these you must simply know you need to maintain.

One of my rhythms has been reading through the Bible each year. I have done this for many years now and have appreciated the insight that I have gained in looking at the entire story of scripture every year. I don't necessarily get caught in the minute details during these readings but simply take a bird's eye view. I don't always feel like doing my daily reading, I often don't think I'm getting anything out of it, especially when I am plowing through some of the OT books, and yet I have learned to not allow myself to make an excuses but to simply do what I know is beneficial for the long term.

As a leader, I don't have someone asking me if I've read the current day's portion, I don't have someone carving out the time I need to make it happen, I've simply had to make it a reality that I will not deviate from. This is what leaders do: they first and foremost lead themselves.

As I recently read in my daily reading, even before the Israelites were led out of Egypt, God was giving them rhythms to live by. The Passover meal was established. "You must remember this day forever. Each year you will celebrate it as a special festival to the Lord" Exodus 12:14. This was only the first of many such daily, weekly, monthly and annual rhythms that God was helping them establish. And why? "Otherwise, when you eat and are satisfied, when you build fine houses and settle down, and when your herds and flocks grow large and your silver and gold increase and all you have is multiplied, then your heart will become proud and you will forget the LORD your God, who brought you out of Egypt, out of the land of slavery" Deuteronomy 8:12-14.

I have watched far too many people become financially successful and forget God, and then when life goes off-track, they all of a sudden discover how important these rhythms are. Yet, once life gets back on track, the rhythms also disappear. A leader of others must not succumb to this.

As you lead others, they are looking to you to demonstrate how a disciple of Jesus stays the course. Find your rhythms, stick with them, and establish a life that will not be shaken.

Matthew

KEEP LEARNING

Dear Garret,

The life of the disciple is that of a learner. You don't know everything and never will, but you don't stop learning.

One of the important aspects of leading well is to always have a teachable spirit. Once you think that you are fully competent, you are heading down a slippery slope. Yes, you are helping someone else become a disciple of Jesus and you will have more insight than those you are leading in many areas pertaining to discipleship, this is given. Yet you can never become complacent in what you know and stop stretching to know more, to gain wisdom.

"Tune your ears to wisdom, and concentrate on understanding. Cry out for insight, and ask for understanding. Search for them as you would for silver; seek them like hidden treasures. Then you will understand what it means to fear the Lord, and you will gain knowledge of God" Proverbs 2:2-5 (NLT). You can't beat Proverbs for talking straight!

As you know, I have personally worked through the same curriculum with the different guys I have been journeying with for years now. I have reviewed the same lessons, talked about the same scripture memory verses, read the same articles. Yet each week before I bring the guys together, I need to sit down, reflect on the material again, and ask God to reveal to me more, to determine what I still do not know and have not yet applied to my life and how this material relates to these students specifically. I must ensure that I bring a posture of teachability.

However, beyond this, I can't simply rely on this material. I need to go beyond, and model what it means to be a lifelong learner. I need to be memorizing new scriptures, reflecting on new passages, reading new books. It can never end.

Now I fully recognize that we each learn in different ways. You need to find the way that you learn best and keep it up, but never stop. One phrase I often use with the guys I'm working with is, "You can't live on last year's information forever, there is more to know."

I have personally enjoyed formal education as a way that I learn well. You know that I have completed both a Masters in Theology and a Doctor of Ministry degree. My thesis title was "Transformative Journeys: An Eight-Month Engagement of Integrated Discipleship Through Service Learning". Yeah, not too exciting, and it won't be on the best-sellers list. However, there were seven conclusions that I drew from this research that are applicable to our desire to see others become disciples of Jesus.

Over the next few letters, I'd like to share them with you. I trust that they will add to your knowledge base.

One of the reasons I'm enjoying writing these letters to you is that they are helping me on my journey as I trust they are helping you. For me there is something about having to articulate my thoughts that make them stick. So as I let you into the heart of my thesis, it is my prayer that you will grow, but know that I am learning right alongside you.

Matthew

REFLECTION

Dear Garret,

Here we go. As I mentioned in my last letter, I want to share with you the conclusions that I came to as a result of my doctoral research. These ideas may not be hugely revelatory, yet for me they were profound as they reinforced some of my thinking with respect to discipleship.

The first is this: Reflection increases life transformation.

One aspect of the project involved a learning model called "Service Learning." Currently being used in an increasing number of universities and colleges, it blends both in-class learning as well as hands-on action that emphasizes what is being taught.

Personally, one of the fascinating parts of this learning style that spoke to me was the aspect of regularly reflecting on the learning that was taking place. The research that has been done on this learning model indicates that unless the student pauses to intentionally reflect (both individually and in a group) on what they are learning, the stickiness of the learning is very limited. With reflection, the learning increases by up to 80%.

We all need to take advantage of the benefits of reflection. Jesus often pulled his disciples aside from the crowds to reflect on what they had been involved with. He would also interact with them around the parables that he had been telling to the crowds, reflecting on the fuller meaning.

For me personally, as someone who is on the go and trying to make things happen, I find that pausing to reflect will only happen if I discipline myself to do this. It has become more of a natural occurrence in the past couple of years, but I do recall how I had to become convinced that it was a good idea so that I would set aside time to reflect.

I was away this past weekend and had a few chunks of time to myself. I knew that I needed to take advantage of this opportunity to reflect. On one occasion, I spent an hour walking along the waterfront reflecting on some memory verses that I'll be engaging in with a group of guys I'm meeting with. I allowed myself to be drawn into them, to be challenged by them, and to be open to whatever the Holy Spirit may want to be teaching me. The more I reflected, the deeper it got, and the more transformative the time became.

As we lead others on this journey of discipleship, we need to become convinced that reflection is beneficial, to allow reflection to become part of a regular pattern of our lives, and then to show those we are leading. This is easily done using scripture, specifically the memory verses you are engaging with. It can also be done with some great questions: What is one thing you liked about last week, what made you angry last week, what are you learning about your children these days? There are thousands of questions that you could come up with. The point is to get those you lead to stop and reflect that they too will learn to embrace this very meaningful discipline.

Life is moving along, the same pace it always has, and yet our choices to fill the time have increased dramatically. To lead well means to choose those aspects that are life giving and to model it for others.

May you choose the slow discipline of reflection – you won't be disappointed.

Matthew

TIME FOR TRANSFORMATION

Dear Garret,

Thanks for your feedback from my last letter. I recognize that as an introvert taking time by yourself may come more naturally for you than it does for me. You are blessed. Yet I know many introverts who will spend time by themselves to reenergize and yet they simply fill their alone time with random and meaningless activities, no focussed reflection. This is important.

Now, let me take you to the second, and perhaps most basic conclusion from my research: Life Transformation Takes Time.

Before you roll your eyes at me for stating the obvious, take stalk of your own learning experiences: how many seminars have you attended, at church or work, where the learning truly took hold and you changed? How many messages have you listened to that intrigued you and yet when the next week's message came you hadn't made any changes? How many times do you offer to go for coffee with a friend to try and help them solve a problem and you wonder why they don't just make the changes you suggest?

The process of life change takes time, lots of time. The commitment to help someone begin the journey of discipleship is also long, and one meeting won't do it. A weekend seminar won't make it happen.

I need to continually remind myself that everyone is on a journey, that many if not most lessons are hard fought as our own self-reliance, pride and ego get in the way of absorbing and implementing whatever life-change God has for us.

I catch myself often wanting those I am working with to just "get it," to catch up to me in what I am learning, only to have one of them make a significant life change decision that I realize I have yet to fully grasp. Maybe I need to catch up to them.

"The Kingdom of Heaven is like treasure hidden in a field. When a man found it, he hid it again, and then in his joy went and sold all he had and bought that field. Again, the Kingdom of Heaven is like a merchant looking for fine pearls. When he found one of great value, he went away and sold everything he had and bought it" (Matthew 13:44-46).

How much time does it take for someone to be so enamored with the Kingdom of Heaven that they will do whatever it takes to be fully part of it? Oh, I realize that many people have epiphanies during a service or at an event and they leave with a conviction that they are going to give their life to God, only to have life hit them in the face on Monday morning at work and it dwindles away. I don't want to question their experience, yet it takes time to build a foundation under that revelation for it to be life changing.

I am learning patience as I work with others. I am learning to enjoy watching the process. It is exciting when a light goes on and someone realizes the impact of a scripture verse, or makes a significant commitment to their marriage, or makes a hard decision at work that is truly kingdom inspired.

I know that I want to embrace the enjoyment of time. Jesus spent close to three years with his core disciples, day in and day out. Interestingly, when he left them, they still didn't think that they were ready, but he knew they were. Besides, he was leaving them the Holy Spirit.

As you embrace the journey of discipleship, as you spend time with those you are leading, enjoy the journey, take the time. After all, God is still working on you.

Matthew

SCRIPTURE

Dear Garret,

Let's look at the aspect of scripture when it comes to the life of the disciple and life-change. This was another component that stood out strong in my doctoral work. Another one of those obvious conclusions perhaps, but it amazed me as to what took place. Never underestimate the importance of scripture.

As part of my project, I provided the opportunity for people to engage with social issues in our city that involved serving alongside non-profit organizations. Along with hands-on serving, we met on a monthly basis. These meetings included learning about a specific issue (i.e. homelessness) from experts in the field as well as reflecting on various scriptures such as Isaiah 58 and the parable of the Good Samaritan.

During the participant interviews that pertained to my research, several of the participants indicated to me that they were only coming for the learning about the service opportunities – these interviews occurred before the initiative began. They didn't believe the scriptural reflecting would impact them that much since they had grown up in the church and knew it all. In some ways I believed them. These were veterans of the church and had heard so many messages and read and studied the Bible for years, was there really anything for them to learn.

Wow, were they wrong! Not from my perspective, but from their own admission. After the eight month initiative was over, I interviewed a number of them as a follow up to understand how the experience influenced them. To a person, they described the impact that the scriptural reflection had had on their lives, impact that they had not expected. They were amazed at the power it had to change their hearts and how it made them read the Bible differently.

Unfortunately, I see too many so called discipling relationship that limit the input of scripture. They read books about the Bible, or books with special interest topics or by the latest Christian writer, but don't simply have the rawness of scripture in front of them.

Perhaps the leader is bored of looking at the Bible, or wants to explore other topics of interest to them. That may be fine at times, yet the role of the leader is to bring into focus the building blocks that any disciple of Jesus needs for long term health and growth.

Scripture is one of the foundational aspect of any life-giving discipling relationship, always has been, always will be. Scripture does change lives. Do you believe it?

Remember this verse that we memorized: "All scripture is God-breathed and is useful for teaching, rebuking, correcting and training in righteousness, so that the person of God may be thoroughly equipped for every good work."

How about this one: "How can a young person stay pure? By obeying your word. I have tried hard to find you— don't let me wander from your commands. I have hidden your word in my heart that I might not sin against you."

Feel free to supplement any discipling relationship with other materials, both written, audio and video. But always remember, your role is to set someone up for long-term stability and growth. The latest author may have some neat things to say, but books with their latest ideas will come and go, they will tickle the mind only for a season.

Without the foundation of scripture and the belief that it is a core component, you will not set people up for the long haul. Don't underestimate the importance of the foundation of scripture. Painting walls that aren't set on a firm foundation is foolishness.

Matthew

COMPLEXITY

Dear Garret,

You asked a great question when we met yesterday, which had to do with what single activity in the discipling journey stands out as more important that the others. You and I are both aware of individuals who, with good intentions, seem to highlight one aspect of the Christian life over others. For some we can't pray enough, and to them there are specific ways the one must pray. Others seem to think that serving the disadvantaged is most important. Others want ongoing Bible studies, to be able to parse verbs and grasp the deep meaning of every noun. So what is it? Great question.

So here is my answer. The one aspect of discipleship that I am discovering more and more is the importance of the integration of multiple activities. Sorry to disappoint. Yet this came clear in my research for my thesis.

The initiative that I had people participate in included personal and group reflection, engagement with scripture, "classroom" learning about a specific need in our city and then hands-on practical service in that area of learning. Everyone that I interviewed at the end of the initiative all agreed that no one activity stood out as more important in their growth. That all of the activities worked together to shape them during the eight-month initiative.

Reflecting on the interactions Jesus had with his disciples, you realize that there were times to pause and learn, and often Jesus pulled them aside for some great teaching moments. However integrated into this were times of active participation in hands-on ministry. Many times the teaching moments came out of the active ministry they had just participated in.

While the cultural context allowed for Jesus and his followers to be together continuously, we need to ask what our cultural context will allow.

I've had several conversations with individuals the past few months who have been involved in varying types of discipleship groups. One of the themes that I have been hearing is that their study is becoming dry. The constant input of information, as good and scriptural as the content is, is feeling like it is missing meaning, an outlet to practice.

For the past number of years, I have been integrating some intentional service with the guys I've been meeting with as I did with you. Whether it is serving breakfast regularly at the homeless drop-in, building picnic tables for a ministry or serving on a non-profit board of directors, these tangible activities have given a context with which to live out our faith. We've learned about each other as we've watched different abilities shine and personality traits be exposed.

We've learned about aspects of concern in our city that we wouldn't have seen otherwise, and our hearts have been exposed to the work of the Kingdom that God is calling us to.

God became flesh and dwelt among us. We too, while we learn to understand God from scripture and through the Holy Spirit speaking to us, must engage practically in the work of the kingdom. These various aspects however must not be done in silos. They work together in the context of a discipling relationship. It may appear more complex, and it is definitely not as convenient, but I believe that discipleship calls us to embrace the complexity of it all.

Matthew

THEOLOGICAL THINKING

Dear Garret,

I have often wondered how a theological textbook would read if it was written by someone who is homeless, or disabled, or has been unemployed for many years, or a housewife, or…

Most theological books I've come across have been written by middle class, white males. Surely they have filters that don't allow them to see the full picture.

Growing up solidly middle-class myself, I am shocked that it took me until age forty to grasp the obvious call to care for the disadvantaged in my very own community. Now that my filter has changed, I can so clearly see the numerous passages, both OT and NT, which not only encourage me on this, but command me to do this. I wonder what other aspects I am missing that in reality should be blatantly obvious.

One of the amazing benefits of this journey is the recognition that moving outside of my comfort zone with people who are different from me is transformative theologically.

How much are you moving beyond your core group of relationships? Do you engage with other people? These will be people who are different from you economically (both poorer and wealthier), politically, denominationally (if we even know what that means anymore), gender, race, religion, occupation, culture, education, etc.

To disciple people who are similar to me is a fairly simple process in many respects. We already think very much alike and we will find ourselves nodding in agreement more often than not.

However, those that I am discipling, if I am to lead them well, we need to move outside of our comfort zones. What we read together, where we serve together, are all important aspects of the journey.

I want them to feel uncomfortable at times, have them squirm. At the same time, they need to see me become uncomfortable and wrestle with my beliefs. Without this, we become stale.

Not that my beliefs are going to be swayed by every new idea that comes my way. Yet it is important to engage with different points of view that may alter my beliefs and practices, or perhaps simply further solidify the beliefs and practices I have.

I recall one of the interviews I had with a participant in my research. She was working with the homeless and was quite engaged in the volunteer work she had chosen to do. At one point in the interview she looked at me as said, "I am so mad at them. Why can't they just get a job and get on with life?" Then, without missing a beat, she responded, "I love them so much. They are so lost and simply need to know that they are loved." She was being pushed and stretched all at the same time. You can be sure that she looked at scripture a lot differently after these encounters.

We can't hide in a protective bubble and simply engage with books and people who will tell us what we want to hear. We don't have all the answers. We aren't living the perfect life.

Let's be sure to move beyond ourselves for our own growth, as well as those we are leading. There is nothing to be afraid of, just transformation waiting to take place.

Matthew

UNIQUENESS OF EACH PERSON

Dear Garret,

As much as I espouse having some pre-set activities for every discipling relationship that I engage with (scripture memory, prayer, curriculum, serving), I must always recognize that each person is unique and that their journey as such will be unique. If I don't keep this before me, I will treat each person as though they were on an assembly line and fail to see how they have been created individually.

I have probably made more errors on this aspect than any other over the years. I am forever thankful for some of the great guys that I have had the privilege of leading who were bold enough to push back when they felt that I was not engaging with them in ways that were meaningful to who they were. It is during those moments that you must be willing to eat humble pie, learn from those you are leading, and make adjustments to the journey.

It is also important to keep in mind that these differences come in a variety of forms.

There are personality differences. Some individuals have deeper sensitivities to various aspects of the journey while others are less so. Some find security in structure and a clear agenda while others are freer flowing in their approach. Some look for the many details, while others are looking to see the big picture learning. None are wrong, just different.

Beyond personality, there are different passions. This becomes obvious with the various topics you will cover. Some will naturally engage in certain topics simply due to their passions. Be conscious that you can learn to understand some topics more intimately when you hear someone with a deeper passion for it talk about it and how they see it impacting themselves and the world.

Family situations are also huge factors in the discipling relationship. Someone who is in the middle of raising children in elementary school will approach things much differently than a single twenty-two year old. Someone working through marriage difficulties will see aspects of God differently than someone who is enjoying a vibrant marriage relationship.

There is also a person's academic bent. Some enjoy reading and study while others were happy that they made it through high school; books just aren't their thing.

All of these differences should not in any way completely sway the discipling process. We all need to be stretched outside of our comfort zones for learning to take place. Yet as you lead others, always be aware of the uniqueness of each individual. Leverage who they are, learn from each of them yourself, and you will enjoy the variety of the body of Christ.

Matthew

MESSY JOURNEY

Dear Garret,

When you choose to come alongside someone in a discipling relationship, I think that you already recognize up front that this is not going to be a straight road with consistent growth each and every week. It just doesn't work that way.

I often wonder if my life would be a lot easier if I simply took the path of conducting weekend seminars on discipleship and met with people now and again for one-off conversations about their relationship with Jesus. I think life would be a lot simpler. I could avoid the messy conversations. I could avoid seasons of dryness when it appears (note: appears) that there is no growth taking place and that perhaps we are simply going through the motions. I could avoid having to talk through ongoing issues and pain as they get worked through. I could avoid having to pick someone up and give them ongoing encouragement to stay the course, that in the end, it will all be worth it.

Yet that isn't how it works. Discipleship is confusing, messy and often uncomfortable, both for the person you are coming alongside and for yourself as well. Remember, your journey of growth never stops either; you are bringing it into the relationship with you.

So the question is not whether it will be confusing, messy and uncomfortable, the question is how I will respond when these aspects are blindingly evident.

The easy thing to do would be to give up, chalk it up to the other person's unwillingness to get it or having an unwillingness to want to step in and grow. Typically though, that isn't the case. In fact, it is during the confusing, messy and uncomfortable times that the most amazing growth is taking place; you simply need the stamina to push through to the other side, both you and the person you are journeying with.

I recall a situation when the two guys I was meeting with were both dragging themselves into our weekly gathering. Verses weren't memorized, the work was barely looked at, and our prayers seemed ineffective. I felt as though I had to carry them from week to week, encouraging them to stay the course. It so happened that we couldn't meet for two weeks, I can't remember why, but I think I was happy to have a break from these "lazy, no commitment, guys" (Sorry, just being honest).

Interestingly, it is during these times when I start to consider whether or not we should continue. As I've shared with you before, I'm not one to drag someone along for too long, there needs to be commitment on both sides. It's also times like these when I wonder if any life-on-life discipling relationships are worth it, are my efforts all for naught.

When we resumed getting together there was a whole new atmosphere. They were engaged, they had made new commitments to the journey. They realized that they had not been fully committed prior to our break, yet they both recognized how much this meant to them and the impact it was having on their marriages and parenting. It was as if they needed the dry spell, a time when the commitment of regularly meeting needed to be tested and questioned to understand the life-giving atmosphere that they were a part of. They were reenergized, and so was I.

When you get into this line work of life-on-life discipleship, you'd better be sure why you are doing it. It can't be for the glory or glamour or recognition, because you won't get it. This is tough slugging kingdom work. Slow, steady, methodical, messy, confusing, uncomfortable – add your own words. Yet, after twenty-five years in this business, I can tell you that it's worth it. It is deep, rich, and rewarding.

Commit to pushing through, commit to learning the craft, commit to walking through swamps, commit to getting dirty, and commit to seeing lives changed. It is worth it.

Matthew

PERSONAL CONFESSION

Dear Garret,

The last letters I sent have highlighted the learning from the recent thesis that I wrote for my doctoral studies. Perhaps I was aware of these conclusions before and intuitively knew it, yet having them rise up from my research and then being forced to articulate them was extremely encouraging for me.

There was one aspect that I decided to not put down as a final conclusion in my thesis but simply called it, "Confession of a Researcher." Let me explain.

The research method that I used is known as Narrative Research. It includes hearing people's stories in the midst of real life circumstances. Five individuals had agreed to allow me to include them in my research during the eight month initiative. I interviewed these five individuals before it started to get a base line of where their lives were at. I then interviewed them again after the eight month initiative was over to determine what, if any, life change took place and also what may have led to it.

My confession is this: I had drawn conclusions about two of the people I interviewed right from the start. I wasn't expecting any life change to take place in their lives over the eight months. I had determined that they would be a part of my research that demonstrated that not everyone will learn. Why I thought this exactly I'm not sure, but something about their language and tone led me to this conclusion.

I confess that I was wrong!

In the final interview after the eight months was over, one stated, "This was much more of a spiritual experience than I was ever expecting." This person then went on to describe how the Bible readings we looked at and discussed moved them in ways they were not expecting. At the start they simply thought that they would gain "head knowledge" about the topic to allow them to serve their community in a better way, nothing else. However, through the eight months their heart was moved in unexpected ways.

The other remarked, "If I had to do it over again, I'd spend less time on church committees and more time engaging my community. I thought I knew the Bible, yet I found out that I was missing huge components of it."

My reflex to quickly come to conclusions is not a characteristic that I pride myself in always. Sure, at times it is important as a leader to make decisions to move things forward. However, when it comes to life change, who am I to decide how the Holy Spirit will move? Who am I to think that I can tell what is going on in someone's heart to determine whether or not the soil is ready to receive seed that will reap a huge harvest?

I need to always remind myself to simply be faithful to my calling to go and make disciples. The disciples Jesus chose weren't any other rabbi's choice, yet they changed the world. Who am I to determine how journeying with someone will impact them?

May I always decide that I will take the discipleship journey with others, to provide them what I can, to model what I know, and allow God to be God in the process. It's much more enjoyable that way.

Matthew

LEARNING PROCESS

Dear Garret,

I was chatting with a fellow disciple maker recently, who asked my opinion of a specific curriculum they were hoping to use. It was a study of the book of James that included a great workbook as well as an audio message series to follow along. After talking about it for a bit, the conversation went to the reasons why we do what we do. How would this particular curriculum be beneficial? Would it fulfill the purposes of a disciple maker?

We talked again about the difference between a typical Bible study versus an intentional discipling relationship. As one who is leading another on this journey, it is our ultimate goal to teach someone how to feed themselves spiritually so that they will one day be able to lead others. It is never good enough to pass on information that simply helps someone to understand and respond to the teachings of scripture.

As I have said in the past, I believe it is important to be going somewhere and that a predesigned curriculum can be very helpful in the process. However, how we engage with the curriculum will make all the difference.

So for this particular situation, I encouraged them to use the James study but with a twist. I asked them to first have everyone read the book of James in its entirety and come to the next gathering with their high level thoughts – what did they see, what were they hearing, what impacted them?

Next, they were to look at the study material and the verses it covered and come ready to discuss it.

Only after the discussion were they asked to listen to the audio message, but not before they had had an opportunity to dig into the text for themselves and do the hard work of understanding what it had to say to their life circumstances.

My fear was that by listening to someone else speak on the text, they would never learn to feed themselves, that they would approach their study with the answers already in hand. This will not build a disciple, it will only keep someone in the camp of self-reliance.

We are called to lead others, and one of the indicators over time will be how many people that we have led are able to feed themselves spiritually and help others do the same. Nothing less will do.

Don't take the easy way out. Don't spoon feed. Push, prod and cajole those you are leading to never take short cuts. Help them to do the hard work of learning how to learn, you'll never be disappointed. After all, that's what you have done. Expect nothing less from others.

Matthew

BE A LUCH TO SOMEONE

Dear Garret,

    I recently shared the stage at a conference with my friend, mentor, ministry partner and colleague, Luch. You have met him on a number of occasions when I brought him to our church to teach.

    He delivered one of his passionate talks at the conference of which I too was able to present. It was fun to do it together. In fact, we'll be sharing the stage again in a couple of months along with his wife, Rosetta.

    Luch and I have connected for a long time—more than twenty-five years actually. I was in second year university when I met him at another event where he was speaking. During one of the breaks I told him that I wanted him to journey with me, to teach me how to be a disciple of Jesus. For the next three years, Luch met with me on a regular basis. He taught me the importance of a daily quiet time with God. Actually, he modelled it more than taught it.

    He demonstrated to me the importance of prayer. I recall one occasion in which we walked around one of the sports fields at the University of Guelph for at least thirty minutes praying and talking and looking at scripture as Luch helped me gain insight into a decision I needed to make at the time. As he said, we couldn't gain insight without prayer and he wanted to live that out with me.

On more than one occasion, Luch got annoyed with me and called out my laziness and lack of commitment to the discipleship process. I didn't like him for it at the time, but he was always right. You see, that's what people do when they care about you, they don't want you to settle for second best.

Since those years at the University of Guelph, our paths have crossed on many occasions. Sometimes we go extended periods without connecting, but when we do get together we simply pick up where we left off. We never have a problem going deep on a topic or with each other, we just know that we can trust each other and that we have each other's back.

Since my initial three-year journey with Luch, I've had the privilege of being a "Luch" to a lot of other guys, including you. I've done my best to give to them what I have received. Some of these guys have become great friends like Luch and me. I can trust them fully, I know that they are there for me.

Many of them have chosen to give to others what I gave to them because of what Luch gave to me. You see, it never ends, this process of discipleship always continues to the next generation.

Luch and I love the verse in 2 Timothy 2:2: "And the things you have heard me say in the presence of many witnesses, entrust to reliable men, who will also be qualified to teach others as well."

It's what we do, it's what we will always do.

As you continue on this path of discipling others, you can be sure that you are becoming a "Luch" to others guys. They will look back on their lives, ten, twenty, thirty years down the road and continue speak highly of the investment you made in their lives.

What you are doing is a good thing. You are leaving a legacy of lives. What more do you want? Stay the course, it's worth it.

Matthew

THE HERMENEUTICAL SPIRAL

Dear Garret,

While on my sabbatical, I came across a term that I probably should have been aware of but I wasn't, the hermeneutical spiral. It sounds impressive, I know. I have since read a bit more about it, and although there are slight variations from different writers, the theme is the same: learning is a matter of process, an ebb and flow between several facets of information.

My understanding of this came from a conversation that took place with an older gentleman, a theologian and writer in Colorado Springs. As we sat in his office bouncing ideas around (I felt as though he valued my insight as much as I was valuing his, even though he was probably thirty years my senior – big lesson right there), he drew a spiral on the white board in his office – "the hermeneutical spiral," he said.

He explained that as we read scripture we gain an understanding of the world around us. Then, as we engage the world around us it begins to shape the scripture we are reading. Sometimes it lines up perfectly, other times it doesn't appear to make sense.

Back to the scriptures we go to gain clarity as to what it is saying, then back into the world around us, then back to scripture, the world, and on it goes.

It is only after many iterations of this back and forth do we truly begin to gain a deep and meaningful understanding of scripture as it pertains to the culture we engage with.

I've shared this with you previously, but for me, a personal example I can give is the whole area of serving those who are disadvantaged. My journey began back in 2004 when I memorized Isaiah 58:6-7.

As I started to engage with, serve and befriend those that I never had connected with previously, my thinking began to change. It was difficult at times and confusing. However, the more I read scripture, combined with my increased involvement with the disadvantaged, the more I began to understand how I was completely failing to do what is now so blindingly obvious and the more I have been understanding the ways in which I am to engage them for their benefit and also how not to engage them.

In fact, it is no longer me and them, but us together as friends coming from different lives lived but still made in the image of God. The spiral continues to this day, as it should.

The whole point of it is to learn how to learn.

Learning can be frustrating at times because we want it to be efficient. Give me the Bible verse, tell me what to do, and away I go. Yet in reality that isn't how it works, it is always a process. Our initial understanding is so often not what it must be, or not as deep and robust as it could be.

One of the great things that we can bring to those that we lead is teaching them how to learn. We are not there to simply provide pat answers as that will only keep them as young disciples. If they can learn how to learn, if they develop a desire to dig deeper themselves, then they have truly become a disciple that will never stop growing. This is our task.

However, the only way for us to help others to grasp it is for us to grasp it ourselves. Don't stop learning. Understand that there will always be more to glean from the scriptures as you engage culture. Always be hungry for more—it will never disappoint. Let the hermeneutical spiral guide you.

Matthew

FUNERALS

Dear Garret,

I attended the funeral service for my Uncle Henry the other day. It was a very nice service that honoured him in many ways as several hundred people sat in the pews of the church. I was glad that I attended and had the opportunity to speak with my cousins about their father and our memories growing up.

As a pastor, I have participated in many funerals over the years, both leading as well as an attendee. As I reflect on each of them, in a way I have discovered that attending funerals has become something of a spiritual discipline for me. Strange yet true.

Funerals, if you let them, will always ground you. They will remind you, if you let them, that your life too will come to an end.

They will ask you, if you let them, to think about your own legacy and what people, especially those closest to you, will say when they stand up at the podium or engage in conversations during the meet and greet time.

They will cause you to think about, if you let them, your eternal state and the conversation you will have with God when you enter into the heavenly realm.

They will humble you, if you let them, as you realize that many of the things you are chasing after are really a lie and will never provide you with the happiness that you think they will.

They will also energize you, if you let them, to give your life to something so much bigger than yourself, something that will scare you, move you out of your comfort zone, and yet be so enticing that you can't help but move to engage in.

Spiritual disciplines can take many forms, yet I must always remind myself that they are disciplines. It may be nice to avoid funerals as much as possible because they make me uncomfortable, and yet I would then miss out on the growth that can take place.

So it is with scripture, prayer, journaling, solitude, and mentoring. Just because you don't feel like doing something, doesn't mean you should avoid it.

It was said about Jesus in Hebrews, "Who for the joy set before him, endured the cross, scorning its shame, and sat down at the right hand of the throne of God." We discipline ourselves because of the joy set before us.

This is what you are to model to those you are walking alongside.

As Paul reminded his followers, "imitate me." When you lead someone you are asking them to imitate you. No, you won't be perfect, but don't use that as an excuse. If you don't lead others, who will? You do have something to offer, never forget that.

Engage in spiritual disciplines, no matter how strange or difficult. Be blessed and be a blessing and one day you will hear, "Well done good and faithful servant, enter into your rest."

Matthew

MINIMUM REQUIREMENTS

Dear Garret,

As you are aware, my children are both in university. I realize that your kids aren't too far behind either. You are only a few more years away from an entire new stage of life

As I reflected on this, I realized that to get in, they had to meet some minimum requirements, without which they would not have been accepted. There are many degrees and diploma programs available if you choose to enter university or college, each with its requirements for entrance – MCATs, LSATs, volunteer work, minimum marks, specific high school courses, and on it goes.

I also realized that once they graduate, they will enter the workforce where once again they will face certain barriers and minimum requirements to begin their career.

I think that most of us are okay with people in many careers having to meet certain minimum requirements, otherwise we could be diagnosed incorrectly by the doctor, the bridge we drive over may collapse, the food we eat may make us ill and the counsellor we see may lead us astray.

How about becoming a disciple? How do we approach those that agree to connect with us? Do we take a laissez-faire attitude toward them, or do we have some minimum requirements? And yes, I do recognize that we are all unique and our personalities are different and our learning styles are not the same. Yet, we must always keep in mind that we are committing to help someone grow, and that growth means that they need to stretch. That stretching isn't always all the comfortable, and yet without it they won't grow.

So here is my question: what are your minimum requirements of those you meet with? What will they be required to do? Are you willing to remove someone from your discipling relationship if they don't want to meet the minimum requirements? My personality is such that I may not "feel" as much as others do, so perhaps you may be thinking that I'm mean spirited.

What did Jesus say? "If anyone would come after me, he must deny himself, take up his cross daily and follow." What do you think that really means? He told the rich young ruler to go away until he was ready to sell everything. He looked at Peter and said, "Get behind me, Satan." He scolded Martha for missing out. On and on we could go.

I ask you again, what are your minimum requirements for those that you disciple? What hoops will they be required to jump through? You are giving of your life for the sake of another. Don't you want a return for your efforts?

I have written on the requirements I have developed for the guys that I meet with in previous letters, I don't need to go into that here. But I do want to challenge you with this question. Think about, pray about, and talk about this: what will you require of those that you are willing to give of your life? This is kingdom work, don't take it lightly.

Matthew

DIVERSITY

Dear Garret,

As you know, for the past eight years I have prayed with a group of men at our church every Monday morning from 7:00 to 8:00 a.m. This group ranges from eight to eighteen men. We don't talk about prayer, we don't have a Bible study about prayer—we pray.

Sometimes we pray for each other in smaller groups, sometimes we pray for our church and the various staff and ministries, sometimes we pray for our city, our country and the world.

As you can imagine, we aren't always fully awake when we arrive, and yet we hold it as a priority for our lives.

For me, it has been a great experience for many reasons. First, it starts my week off with some significant prayer, providing a solid foundation to begin the week. There is something good about coming before God with like-minded men in prayer.

More importantly, in the midst of the diversity, it is teaching me to pray. You'd think that after all these years I would know how to pray, and I do. However, I find that there is always something new to learn.

Every man has a style to their praying. Some are elegant in their prose and the words seem to flow out effortlessly. Some are more to the point without any extra words added for definition

– just the facts. Still others seem more disjointed as they try to finds the words to express what is on their hearts. Amazingly, in the middle of this variety, I'm relaxed. I have my style, they have their style. We hear and learn from each other.

Beyond their style, each man has topics of prayer that they tend to emphasize. One man prays for families and marriages, another for the city, one man cares deeply for outreach around the world, still another for the pastors at our church. As I sit in the circle and listen to the many prayers, I get a sense of the importance of community. No one of us cares enough for all aspects of life, but together our prayers encompass so much more. Perhaps God gives each of us a passion so that collectively we are stronger. I feel good about that, more complete.

As I looked around the group last week, I realized that we also represent various cultural groups – first generation Caribbean, Chinese, Syrian, African and Italian, with a few of us Canadians mixed in. Not only do our passions guide our prayers, our cultural formation shapes our prayers.

We don't do life alone. Our faith can never be a private thing, it just doesn't work that way. Sure, doing life with others is messy, uncomfortable and strange at times. Yet, if you step back and look at the richness of the diversity and have a willingness to learn from others, you can't help but be thankful for the beauty of community. This is particularly important for you to model as you lead a few other guys. Embrace each of their unique perspectives and personalities and cultures.

As you lead others on the journey of discipleship, always be mindful to bring them into the larger body of Christ. Don't hide in your small group and think you have it all together, you don't. We do the Church a disservice by being loners and independent thinkers.

There is much to learn from the diversity. Let's lead the way on this.

Matthew

DON'T FACILITATE

Dear Garret,

As you are keenly aware, I'm always very interested in chatting with those who take the next step and choose to disciple others as you have recently done. I'm excited for them and pray for them as their names come to mind. They have begun a great adventure that will not only have a lasting impact on those they lead but on themselves as well.

Interestingly, from time to time I will hear them talk about their experience, either to me or to those that they are connecting with. I am surprised that at times they speak in terms that present themselves as someone who lacks experience, doesn't really have much to offer and are simply facilitating the discipleship process.

Can I provide one word? Nonsense.

I've written to you on this previously but I think it bears repeating. Now hear me out.

You have just begun a relationship with one or more individuals who agreed to allow you to guide them on this journey. Apparently, they sensed in you something that they do not have and they were willing to place themselves under your leadership. They trust you to take them places that they have not been. At the least, you owe them your confidence.

Now let's be honest. You know and I know, and I believe that those you lead know, that you are not perfect. That's a given. You will be learning during this journey just as they are. You will be learning from them perhaps as much as they learn from you. This is all good and normal. In fact, if you aren't learning, then something isn't working.

However I believe that presenting yourself as someone who really doesn't have something to offer is false humility.

Look at it this way: are you personally going to follow someone who presents themselves as less than competent? Think about those you have followed and have listened to for advice. My guess is that you looked up to them and were glad that you met them and were able to glean insight from them. You didn't hold them up or put them on a pedestal as though they were super human. Yet you made changes to your life as a result of the confidence they demonstrated on the topic of conversation.

You are being the same for someone else. Lead boldly; believe in yourself.

Perhaps this sounds like a pep talk for a sports team full of bravado and self-help statements. Perhaps. I honestly believe that as we appreciate our standing under Christ, we can move forward in confidence and believe that we will make a difference in someone's life. The Apostle Paul on one hand spoke of himself as being the worst sinner and yet he also said to those he was leading to imitate him as he imitated Christ. Bold, yet I'm sure also reassuring to those who attached themselves to him.

People want to be led, I'm convinced of that more and more. Even though I am leading others, I am still looking to be led as well by mentors of mine.

As you move forward on this journey, do so with self-belief. You have the opportunity of a life time. You are leaving a legacy. Be excited. Be confident.

Matthew

DEFINING SUCCESS

Dear Garret,

I'm not sure we've discussed this topic in depth but I do believe that it is an important one to address. It has to do with success in discipleship.

It's funny, but when I think about the word success, I am taken back to my high school days and the cheerleading squad that would cheer on the various sports teams. "S-U-C-C-E-S-S, that's the way we spell success. Can we win it, well I guess, Eden Flyers are the best." Then they would repeat it, over and over again, jumping up and down, doing cartwheels and waving pom-poms. Don't you love nostalgia? But I digress.

In sports, success is defined by winning – if you win, you are successful, and if you lose, you are not. I suppose as a team is rebuilding they will look for signs of improvement over time and call that success, but in reality, we all know that success in sports is to win, period.

How would you define success in a discipling relationship? What is a win? Is it even reasonable or worthwhile or biblical to do this? When it is over, when you move on from those you were formally discipling and release them for ministry, how will you know if you were successful?

I've pondered this question over the years. As with any rebuilding sports team, I am always looking for signs of growth, and in a way each sign I see as part of the success, wins along the way. Have their prayers become more about others and not simply their own needs, has the rawness of certain scriptures gripped their lives in unique ways demonstrating an openness to hear from God, has their vulnerability in our relationship grown, have they made positive changes to their various relationships due to the subtle promptings from the Holy Spirit, and on and on. These are all great things and I am excited when I see any one of them taking place.

However for me, these are only markers on the journey to success, they are not the win.

So how do I define success?

Success is when someone I have spent time with in a life-on-life discipling relationship steps out from my council and chooses to come alongside someone else and take responsibility for their spiritual growth as I did for them. It is easy to measure, there are no fuzzy edges to guess at. Someone either is or isn't discipling someone else.

Here is the interesting thing: I believe that after twenty-five years of building into the lives of other guys, that I am about 50% successful. Of all of the guys that I have spent time with, week in and week out, praying with, engaging around scripture, sharing meals, serving together, laughing, crying – half of them decide that this is important enough to do with others while the rest carry on with life.

I have shared this definition with others over the years. Some think that I am being harsh or critical in my definition of success, that I have no idea the impact my discipling relationship has had on the lives of those who perhaps did not choose to take up the mantle of discipleship as I have defined it. That is true. Someone's life will change if they are in a tight relationship for one or two years, no doubt, and I am thankful for that. However for me, the only way that others will gain the benefit of a life-on-life discipling relationship is if those who have experienced it choose to also take up the mantle, there is no other way.

As such, I will continue to hold to my definition of success and continue to work toward increasing my success rate beyond 50%. This is what I will choose to run my race for.

How do you define success?

Matthew

SUMMER VACATION

Dear Garret,

As with you, I am looking forward to summer time here in Ontario. It is a chance for us to get in even more mountain biking runs late into the evening as the day light is much longer.

Isn't it interesting how summer in the colder climates of the world takes on a whole new reality? Yes, this covers pretty much all of Canada. Our American friends think we live in igloos year round. However, the opportunities to be outside, biking, running, camping, vacationing, days at the beach—these all change the rhythm of our lives for a few months each year.

As a pastor, having observed many years of this rhythm from those in our church, I realize that once September comes and everyone returns to the normal routines of life, there will be this reality that many people have had little to no intentional spiritual connecting all summer long. Many attend fewer if any weekend services. Those involved in small groups decide to stop meeting for the summer. Perhaps a barbeque or two will suffice. Kids are rushed around to their sport practices and games while times of prayer or reading scripture are neglected as people attempt live off the spiritual input from the past year.

It should not be this way. As someone who leads others, you need to lead the way on this.

What will you do this summer to engage with God and how will you help those that you are leading to have the same commitment?

As someone who continues to meet with my guys throughout the summer months (Why wouldn't I? It is energizing in so many ways.) I recognize that our weekly consistency does get disrupted at times as we all take some time for vacation which typically means getting out of the city – this is good. I personally just came back from a week away with my wife – 900km away. As we took some time to relax and see new places, I also have come to realize that my time to spend with God in solitude and prayer need not be disrupted in any way. In fact, if I choose to, I can find increased time and more focussed time so that my growth is enhanced not hindered.

I recall a trip we did as a family to Jamaica a number of years ago. We settled into an all-inclusive resort for a week and enjoyed all sorts of great activities including learning how to Scuba dive. However, even in all of the excitement of activities, I was very aware of my desire to enjoy some Sabbath rest and personal time with God. My family knew that for an hour every afternoon, I simply wanted time alone for reflection on scripture, journaling and prayer. Beyond my own personal growth, I was also aware of the importance of my children seeing the significance my faith in God had in my life. This was not a ritualistic thing but something that is alive and vibrant.

In the same way, I'm leading by example the guys that I am coming alongside. When we meet during the summer, what do they observe in my life? Have I taken a vacation from God, or is my relationship with him as dynamic as always?

I don't want to spend every September getting back on track with God as I observe so many doing. Every day, every week, every month, every year—there aren't any pauses to faith, it is interwoven in all aspects of life. Change of seasonal rhythm should always been seen as an opportunity, not a hindrance.

As you journey through these summer months, lead well. This includes leading yourself as well as those that you are developing. May you all enter September with a passion to know God more because of the great times you had in July and August.

Matthew

WHO TO INVEST IN

Dear Garret,

You asked such a great question the other day when we met. The answer to it is also much more art than it is science. The question was this: how do you decide who you will choose to invest in for the purposes of discipleship? By the way, if you ever find the ultimate answer, please let me know.

That being said, let me take a stab at it.

A good friend recently sent me some thoughts titled, "Eight Principles of Discipleship." It outlined many aspects of discipleship, some of which I have touched on in previous letters. However, one stood out for me that was a great reminder and addresses this question.

"True discipleship occurs only when the disciple assumes the primary responsibility for his/her growth."

I had to laugh. How many times have I tried to convince someone that their next step was a deeper relationship with God and that I was willing to walk alongside them? At times some agreed and we would begin the discipling journey together, only to watch their frustration grow at the same rate of my frustration with them. "Why don't they want this?" I would often muse, only to realize looking back that they never really wanted to take responsibility for their growth. They had always been in the mindset of being spoon fed and had no intention of ever making much of an effort to grow in their relationship with God.

I don't in any way want to judge them (unfortunately I often did that in the past) or think of them as less than me.

I don't know why some want to take their relationship with God seriously and some don't. I've had that conversation with God on many occasions. I've had many conversations with people about it as well and they also don't have an answer.

The Spirit moves in ways that we will never fully understand. People choose in ways that we will never fully understand.

A young father with three young children will claim that he is too busy to meet regularly, while at the same time, another young father in the same circumstances will see meeting with someone to disciple him imperative if he is going to be the role model for his wife and children he believes he is called to be. Why two different responses from people in similar situations? I don't know.

That is not for me to decide. It is what it is.

What is for me to decide is who I will choose to spend my time with. I don't want to spend my energy dragging someone along the discipleship road if they have no intention of taking it seriously. It doesn't help either of us.

I want to make sure that I am coming alongside someone who wants to "assume the primary responsibility for his/her growth."

It is September. Many people will have had some time to think over the summer and are ready to take the next step. If they are, we need to be ready and willing to embrace them for this journey. If they aren't, we'll wait for another day. We'll let the Spirit work mysteriously and be ready for when we are called upon.

Matthew

THE FEAR OF CHANGE

Dear Garret,

Let's talk about change, shall we? Are the guys you lead afraid of change? Many people say that they are, and many organizations are often held back because people baulk at change. But is it change they are afraid of or simply the unknown? Is it change or the impact on them personally? Is it change or the moving away from what has become comfortable?

No matter what way you phrase it, I find that many in general are slow to adapt to new realities or to adopt new ways of living.

When it comes to forming ourselves spiritually, we need to convince those we lead that they need to consider change. Not simply change for the sake of change, but change with the intention of stretching spiritual muscles that they haven't stretched in a long time or perhaps never knew they had or maybe muscles that they gave up on, thinking that they really didn't need them.

The change I am talking about is a change to what I like to refer to as Spiritual Disciplines. You obviously recognize these as prayer, scripture reading and study, service, and solitude.

Like all people, you have your preferred array of spiritual disciplines that you engage in as do the guys you are meeting with. This would include some sort of Bible intake (reading a passage and thinking about it, reading a devotional, listening to a message), prayer (by yourself at a set time, mini-prayers throughout the day, weekly with a prayer group), and perhaps a time of worship through singing (typically at a church service although this could include a time of playing a worship CD and basking in the experience).

Though these routines are good, and I recommend maintaining them, how about helping them try something new? How about asking them to experiment with a discipline that is completely outside of their comfort or personality style?

One discipline that I have experimented with over the past few years is solitude; being by myself with no distractions or people to interact with. Dallas Willard pushed me to try this with his definition of solitude when he said that it is simply giving up your kingdom. You give up control of a time. During this time you have no agenda. You don't read, you don't listen to music, you don't even pray—you simply exist with nothing.

If you are like me, this can be painful. I am a doer by nature. To sit still for two hours doing nothing seems like five weeks. The idea of giving up my kingdom, not having any agenda for a period and allowing God to show up in a unique way if He so desires, is a way to recognize that this life is not about me, that I can't allow myself to be a slave to anything but God, whose "yolk is easy and whose burden is light."

A year ago, I went on a four-day retreat at a friend's cottage from Sunday to Wednesday. It was only me. In addition to the loneliness, I also engaged in the discipline of fasting (I love food, no matter the type). My time was not just void; I had significant times of prayer, I read a book, memorized Psalm 101, kayaked around a lake each day, and simply enjoyed nature. I was by myself with no one to talk to, just God and the birds and squirrels around the cottage. I can tell you that by Wednesday I was exhausted (and hungry). It was a draining experience.

Now for some people I know, that experience would have been completely the opposite, it would have energized them. We are all different.

Do I simply stick with what I know, with what works for me, or do I allow myself to venture into spiritual disciplines that will take me to new places and stretch me in new ways? I can tell you that God showed up during that time at the cottage. I was able to intercede in prayer in ways that I had not done in a long time. Memorizing Psalm 101 and playing around with it in my mind continues to impact my life even to this day. Had I not determined to venture into uncommon territory, I would not have experienced this.

Will I, or should I, engage in solitude regularly? I know that I haven't. It isn't my natural bent, and yet I still find time on occasion to be silent for an hour or two, to give up my kingdom.

I leave this challenge with you. As we approach the fall, a time of renewal and new beginnings, will you be willing to step into a new spiritual discipline? Will you allow yourself to walk in uncharted territory? Will you be willing to submit yourself to a different way of approaching your spiritual growth?

As a leader of others, it is your responsibility, or can I say privilege, to lead the way into new ways of approaching life so that we can better assist those we are walking alongside.

Change is good for the soul, we simply need to be courageous to go there. Blessings as you embrace a new reality.

Matthew

IT'S ALL ABOUT THE CORE

Dear Garret,

As you know, I am an advocate of triads. Simply put, this is three people that meet together on a regular basis for the purpose of personal and spiritual growth and development. One of the keys to this is the size of the group. You and I experienced this for two years when we met.

However your question yesterday was a good one. You have up to five guys that are interested in meeting with you, which would make your new group as many as six. What should you do?

Should you simply choose some of the guys and dismiss the others for another time and trust that someone else will pick them up? How important was it to have only three guys? Should you deviate from what you have been committed to the past four years? Are you headed for failure if you have a group of six?

It was a great conversation as we bounced around the pros and cons. I think we realized that in these circumstances, it is imperative that we always go back to the core, to what we are trying to accomplish. We can never let the forms we use become more important than the reason we meet in the first place.

Honestly, a group of five or six may work, in fact, a group of eighty could work if every single person was fully committed, self-motivated, and willing to go deep relationally as they trust everyone with who they are and had each other's best interest at heart.

How often have you heard the phrase, "we've always done it this way?" How many churches are dwindling to nothing simply because they want to hold on to a way of "doing church" that no longer connects within this cultural context?

My encouragement to you is simple: go for it. As you do, be constantly aware of the dynamics and how the guys are maturing in their faith. Try to understand what is working well and what isn't. Make changes as necessary and if it doesn't work out, don't worry about it. Take courage in the fact that you kept the main things the main things and that you were willing to step out and try something beyond what was the norm for you.

We need to always ask questions about what works and what doesn't. We need to always try new things to help others mature in their faith in God. We must never become so tied to what is working today that we miss what will work in the future. Maintain the core purposes of what you are trying to accomplish and experiment always with the forms to get there.

Matthew

MORE THOUGHTS ON REFLECTING

Dear Garret,

As you know, our church recently developed a reflection exercise. It provides a simple process for someone to think through the various aspects of their life to determine where they believe they need to put some concerted effort into personal growth and development.

I was a key player in putting this together and then rolling it out. Honestly, I hope that maybe 10% of those who received it will actually take the time to work through it. That's not a high number by any means, but if some begin to pause to reflect then perhaps over time others would see the impact that it had on their life and desire it for themselves. I'm a realist in these things. Experience tells me that people don't like to reflect on their lives.

My wife and I both went through it and spent some time over dinner one evening letting each other know what we discovered. For me it was good to articulate back to her what I was thinking and what I believed to be some of my next steps of growth.

By way of modelling, let me share with you my own reflection results and what I believe I need to spend time focussing on the next six months or so.

Interestingly, my growth landed in the area of home, specifically my marriage and my parenting.

As I shared with Janice, I want our next twenty-three years of marriage to be so fun and engaging that the first twenty-three years would appear pale in comparison. Specifically, I decided that I needed to stop nit-picking her in some areas. It just wasn't fair to her and frankly it did nothing to help her or enhance our relationship. I won't give specifics here but I did give her some concrete examples.

How am I going to do this? First, I told her, so she knows my desires. Second, I've told others including the guys I'm meeting with so they can hold me accountable. Third, we are going to attend the marriage seminar that our church is hosting this fall. I believe that these three things will go a long way in helping me to take steps forward on this.

The second area of growth for me is in parenting. My children are twenty and eighteen, and both are in university. My twenty-year-old son is married and so I now also have a daughter-in-law. How do you parent children at this stage of life? I don't think you can simply hope it all works out well; there needs to be some intentionality. Looking back on the past six months to a year, I think I have already missed unique opportunities. I need to grow in this.

So what am I doing? At this point in time, I have begun to have conversations with others who are ten or more years beyond me on this journey. I ask them what they learned, what they did well and what they would have done differently. I trust that I will be able to gain insight and be the father that I believe I need to be and that my children want.

As one who leads others, we all need to take the time to reflect on our lives. We need to be continually increasing our awareness of where our gaps are so that we can live lives that reflect Christ to those we lead and those we connect with.

Reflecting isn't always easy. It often reveals things that we simply don't want to know about, and yet, left unchecked, these areas may be our downfall.

Let's decide that we will do the hard work of looking in the mirror, honestly recognizing where we need to grow, and then taking practical steps to bring about change. It's worth it.

Matthew

DON'T LEAD LIKE JESUS

Dear Garret,

I had the privilege of speaking to a group of pastors this past week on the area of discipleship. It's a topic that probably keeps many of them awake at night.

I began the talk with three things that we need to admit about discipleship to get the conversation started and hopefully to challenge accepted ways of thinking that I believe are not right. I'd like to share these with you over the next few letters and trust that it will push our thinking in new ways.

To get things started the first admission was this: we need to admit that we cannot disciple the way that Jesus did. It's a great way to begin a talk on discipling people to live like Jesus, and it got their attention.

Interestingly, I received an email the morning of the talk. It was promoting a conference that stated the following: "Founded on the process of disciple-making that Jesus taught and modeled, [this conference] will teach how He turned fisherman and tax collectors into some of the most influential men ever to live". Really? It sounds very spiritual and noble, that we are able to read the Bible and take the practical methods of Jesus and apply them today. But really?

Let's admit that it is culturally impossible to makes disciples like Jesus did, that Jesus simply used the culturally relevant methods of his day. These methods will NOT work in our context. In fact, unless you are ready to choose twelve teenage boys and live with them for three years and then have yourself killed so that they are forced to carry on the work, then we cannot disciple like Jesus did.

Why do we think that talking spiritually about how Jesus did things makes things better? Jesus lived in a cultural context that involved Rabbis and disciplees – it was normal for this to happen. That is not normal for today. In fact I believe that we have more to learn from general research on adult learning than we do from the methods used in scripture. There is nothing wrong in admitting this. Being a disciple of Jesus simply means to be a learner of Jesus' way of life. How do we learn best?

This fall I committed myself to spending three hours each week at our university library reading books and taking notes on adult learning methods. I truly want to help others in their walk of faith and I'll only be able to do this best by learning how people learn in my context, not in a context from two thousand years ago.

Call me a heretic if you'd like, but I'd like to think of myself as constantly trying to be relevant.

I typically work with guys who are involved in business. My wife is involved with young women who struggle with certain social issues but still want to follow Jesus. Do you think it looks the same when we get together? Absolutely not.

We have the privilege of walking alongside people to help them follow Jesus with all of their heart, mind and strength. Let's do that, where they are at, and in a way that is relevant.

Matthew

DISCIPLESHIP IS NOT SIMPLE

Dear Garret,

I shared with you in my last letter my first in three admissions that I believe we need to make about discipleship. The second admission is this: discipleship is not simple.

We are part of a large church where I am a pastor. In fact, I work with twelve pastors. Close to two thousand people come through the church doors every weekend to attend one of four services. It is a diverse church demographically, from infants to seniors and everyone in between. In many ways, it has been able to maintain a strong connection to all ages and stages. This is a good thing.

As you know, my job title is Pastor of Adult Discipleship. Basically, this covers everything to help adults grow in their walk with God outside of the weekend service experience, including electives, seminars, small group ministry, and mentoring relationships.

Do you know what would be nice? Do you know what would make my role efficient? Do you know how I could guarantee that everyone in our church would grow together and impact our city and the world?

If everyone would line up and simply follow the five-step process that I develop and come out the other end fully prepped and ready to be the fully devoted follower of Jesus that I have mapped out for them.

You can stop rolling your eyes at me. I don't have a five-step plan mapped out and I often question whether I really know what a fully devoted follower of Jesus looks like or does.

Can we admit that discipleship is not simple, that it never has been and never will be?

There is a book that came out in 2006 called *Simple Church: Returning to God's Process for Making Disciples*. Huh? First of all, read my previous letter and you will understand what I think about the tag line for the title of this book.

But Simple Church? Where does this come from? I do know of some churches that have adopted this model and I just don't get it. Personally, I think it is more a response from pastors who don't want to do the hard work of discipleship but would rather move people around like pawns or widgets and track it on a database. I don't want to discount the work that they are doing in any way, but I think I need to challenge their thinking.

Let me say it again: Discipleship is not simple. In fact, it is probably one of the most complex things you can engage in, since we are not only coming alongside people to help them follow Jesus, be we also have to fight "against evil rulers and authorities of the unseen world, against mighty powers in this dark world, and against evil spirits in the heavenly places" Ephesians 6:12 NLT.

Why do we think that we can line people up, send them through a production line and have them come out the other side changed? Why do we think that attending a service each weekend, being in a small group of 8-12 people, having a prescribed devotional time each morning and serving once a month where the church tells you to serve is the formula for maturing in faith?

Look, I am a big advocate of spiritual disciplines and faith routines – they have been a lifeline to me on many occasions. I know that I have developed some methods that I have been using to come alongside other guys for many years. I have had a fair bit of success with this (I use that term loosely).

For me as a pastor to lay out a linear path of discipleship for the two thousand people at my church to go through and expect maturity, I'm only fooling myself and them.

The process is messy, winding, and confusing. Instead of getting frustrated with this, I simply need to embrace it. This is reality. Life is not linear. If you want neat and tidy and organized, then work in a factory and make widgets. If you want to help lives be changed, jump into the swamp and start swimming. It's a blast.

The work that you are doing is rich. You are coming alongside a couple of guys and "doing life" with them. You are living through the ups and downs of their growth. Keep it up. It is good work.

Matthew

DO WHAT YOU ALREADY KNOW IS RIGHT

Dear Garret,

So here is my third admission: We know what we need to do, so why don't we do it?

Back in 2006, our church was looking at developing a formal leadership training program to see if we could enhance our capabilities in more effectively guiding others. As part of the pre-work, I was asked to interview a number of leaders (both paid and volunteer) to understand what they did to improve their leadership capabilities and why they believed they took on Christian leadership roles in the first place.

The conversations were engaging and I heard many thought-provoking ideas. Interestingly, as I gathered my information, there was one overriding theme that came through from almost all of the leaders. Each one of them highlighted the fact that early in their lives someone came alongside them and mentored them, both in their faith journey as well as issues of life in general. Typically, it was meeting with them on a weekly basis, often times for up to two years, and many of these leaders were still in contact with those mentors. As someone who has been doing this for many years, I was excited by this finding.

When I heard this, I asked a follow up question: since this life-on-life connecting had had such a big impact on their lives, who were they meeting with so that this could be passed on to the next generation? It only made sense that if this was instrumental in their lives then they would want to do the same for someone else.

Every single one of them replied, "no one." Did you hear that? "No one."

The very thing that had laid the foundation for their lives and set them on a course of leadership, the one thing that everyone had recognized as being instrumental in their own development, they were not doing themselves.

I had to ask myself, why did we need to develop any leadership development program? What would its purpose really be? The leaders that we had already knew what they needed to do to develop leaders. Each of them had been given a gift from someone else who had come alongside them to develop them. All they needed to do was to do the same thing with some else and the leadership development circle would continue.

Church leaders continue to look for methods and programs and formats that they believe will help those in their congregations to grow and mature. They change things up on a regular basis trusting that one of these years they will find the magic bullet. Yet, people continue to live stagnant lives when it comes to faith in God.

Can we admit that we already have the methods and means with which to help others grow and develop? We don't need the next great DVD series from the next up and coming communicator of the fastest growing church in North America. We don't need to find another set of curricula to use. We don't need to attend yet another conference on the latest relevant religious topic.

Think about your own development and growth. What was it for you? Was it fancy and earth shattering? Did it involve massive gatherings of people in convention centres? This may have played a small part, and yet, what was it really?

Personally, I agree with the leaders that I interviewed. A guy came alongside me in second year university and I met with him on a consistent basis. We memorized scripture, we prayed, we studied. He shared his life with me and helped me figure out mine.

We are still friends to this day.

Perhaps there is nothing exciting about this, and yet, when I look back on my life, it set the course for the last twenty-five years, and that is very exciting.

Let's admit that we know what we need to do to make disciples. It's not complicated. Let's get on with it and do what we know we need to do.

Matthew

FRAGILE

Dear Garret,

It was fun connecting the other night with our wives. It is always encouraging when our wives are also engaged in the same work that we are in. There is an understanding of the joys and complications in the life of a disciple maker that can only enhance your marriage.

As we drove home, my wife and I had a great conversation. We were discussing the initial stages of the process when we are only a few months into the journey of intentionally connecting with those we are helping. As we were bouncing around ideas about the fun as well as the complications of these first few months, she said to me, "It is so fragile."

As I heard that word, I could only nod in agreement. It is a great word to describe it. As we talked more, we realized that the fragility was seen in those we are coming alongside as well as in ourselves. Perhaps you have experienced this.

There is a bit of a dance that takes place at the start of a discipling journey. As much as someone has agreed to allow us to lead them, and as much as we have tried to be fully honest in what our expectations are, they simply don't know what they don't know. They really don't know what they are getting themselves into. This includes the time commitment as well as the life change that will take place, which can be uncomfortable at time.

After the conversation, I reflected on some of the people that I have journeyed with over the years.

I have connected with a number of guys that started out strong and appeared fully committed, and yet, within a few months, it was over. They lost interest. There were other life priorities that kept coming up. Questions I asked appeared to poke around in places in their lives that they just didn't seem to want to talk about. The journey ended before it really began.

Others I have met with appeared to be confused at the start, and I questioned right away whether they would make it. They had questions about life and shared things about what they believed that left me wondering whether they would stick around that long. Their current experiences and beliefs made me wonder about their faith and whether it would be a long journey of doubts and questions for their own sake without a desire to truly mature in faith. It is during these times that I simply listen and allow them to speak. Inside I wonder when I need to push them in a new direction and when I simply need to hold back and let the Holy Spirit do what only he can. If I interject too soon, I might ruin a journey of faith. If I hold back too long without challenging where I believe I need to, I am failing to lead as I believe I am called to.

It is during these moments that you realize how fragile the situation is.

I have come to appreciate the parable of the Sower and Seed in deeper ways over the past few years. It describes so well these situations. You can read it in Luke 8. The seed is being spread and begins to germinate, but at times the sun withers it up, or the worries of this world choke the plant, or at times the devil comes and takes the seed away even before it has a chance to take root. The seed appears to be so fragile.

I wish I had the simple solution to these fragile times. I wish there was a science to understanding what it is all about and the three steps to take to make sure that someone stays on track. But I've learned that it is not that simple. It is something you simply need to learn over time through trial and error. Believe me, I have had my share of errors in this area. Some guys have been gracious with me as I have learned, others not so.

When you experience this, I simply encourage you to stay with it. Keep praying for discernment. Maintain a heart that is truly wanting the best for each person you are discipling. If it doesn't go as planned, don't beat yourself up. Learn what you can learn, be open to the Holy Spirit speaking to and molding you personally, and get back in the game.

Matthew

DEAR READER OF "LETTERS TO GARRET",

I'm not sure why you chose to read through these letters. My guess is that you fall into one of three categories of people.

First, you may be someone who has never even given much thought to coming alongside someone but someone gave you this book to read. Perhaps you don't believe you are capable. Perhaps you have always thought that it was the role of your pastor or someone with a theology degree. Maybe you have never even heard of life-on-life discipleship and your only understanding of someone growing in their faith was to attend a weekly service at a church and attend a seminar or conference from time to time.

Let me encourage you to think differently. I trust that reading through these letters has given you a new perspective on what assisting someone in their relationship with God might look like. If you have been a Christian for more than five years, perhaps your next step is to come alongside another and journey with them. Not only will you be helping them grow, but you will find that your own maturity will increase exponentially.

Second, you may be someone who has considered coming alongside someone but you just haven't taken the next step. Perhaps fear has stopped you. Maybe you are waiting for someone to ask you, or possibly you are trying to figure out how it will fit in your schedule.

Let me challenge you to not wait any longer. Reading more books or attending another conference won't give you any more insight. You need to simply step in and learn from experience, that is your next step. Don't wait for one of your friends to start. Don't wait for your pastor to ask you. Someone is waiting for you to come alongside them. It is time.

Finally, you may be someone who is in the game. You have committed to building into the lives of a few and are leaving a unique legacy of changed lives. I applaud you. You are doing great work. I recognize that not many people may see the work that you are doing. Those who do may not understand the significance of it either. Perhaps you've even received negative comments from people, even your pastor. Unfortunate, but I've heard too many stories like this. Why some pastors feel threatened by this, I do not understand, but it is reality that I have been told about on more than one occasion.

May I encourage you to stay the course, to continue with the consistent week in and week out work that you are doing. I often tell the guys I'm working with that their growth is an inch a day. You may not even see growth week to week, and yet if you look back six months, you'll definitely see it. You'll particularly notice it if you step out of a discipling relationship for a time.

I believe that life-on-life discipleship is a spiritual discipline, just like prayer, scriptural input, solitude and serving, to name just a few. It is something that Christians must be involved in. I also recognize that not many are doing it. They'd rather continue to be spoon fed, to passively take in content from weekly services and seminars.

Those that choose to take it on are in the minority. Yet the work that they do is of utmost importance.

My prayer is that these letters will spur you on. That you will choose to give your life to this.

Imagine what spiritual growth would look like in your current church context if even 3-5% of those that attended were involved with this work. Imagine the depth of people's relationship with God and with each other.

I challenge you to simply take the next step and do it. Don't wait for your church to set up a program and invite you in. Don't expect your friends to join with you either. Step out, ask two others to join you, and lead. It's the journey of a lifetime.

One day you will hear, "Well done, good and faithful servant."

Matthew
www.matthewweckert.com

ABOUT THE AUTHOR

Matthew Eckert has been engaging in the work of life-on-life discipleship since he was introduced to it back in 1986. First as a university student, then during a 12 year banking career, and now as a pastor, he has always maintained that an important spiritual discipline is to build spiritually into the lives of others providing them with the necessary confidence to do the same. A life-long learner with degrees in science, business and theology, including a Doctor of Ministry from Tyndale Seminary in Toronto, Ontario, Canada, his broad educational and work experience has given him a unique perspective on life and personal development. Matthew and his wife, Janice, currently reside in London, Ontario, Canada.